ROBERT RAIKES
of
GLOUCESTER

ROBERT RAIKES
of
GLOUCESTER

Frank Booth

NATIONAL CHRISTIAN EDUCATION COUNCIL
Robert Denholm House
Nutfield, Redhill, Surrey, RH1 4HW

SB 12455 £6.95 2.80

ISBN 0 7197 0249 6

Typeset by Trident Graphics Limited, Reigate, Surrey
Printed and bound by Staples Printers Rochester Ltd, Kent

TO MY WIFE

CONTENTS

INTRODUCTION

Robert Raikes was one of the leading figures of the eighteenth century. The stories which grew up around him hid his essential greatness as a pioneer not only of Sunday schools but also of popular education.

This book sets out to show Raikes the man within his historical context and to discern something of his work through his own writings in the *Gloucester Journal*, and through the view of his contemporaries.

In writing this book I have been helped by many people and would like to express my thanks to them, particularly to the Staff of the Robert Raikes Reference Library, Gloucester. I am very grateful to Major Duncan Raikes, Professor Brian Simon and Professor W. Roy Niblett for their encouragement and helpful suggestions, and to Mr Brian Frith, Mr T. W. Hearl and Mr Bryan C. Jerrard who kindly read and commented on the manuscript. I wish to pay special tribute to Miss J. Wans without whose enthusiasm and willingness to undertake challenging and laborious tasks the work would not have been completed. All the mistakes, of course, are my own.

F.B.

Chapter 1
RAIKES' ENGLAND

The England of Robert Raikes, founder of the Sunday School Movement, differed greatly from the England we know today, and to understand Raikes' actions, attitudes, and the limitations in his thinking we need to examine the political, social, and religious structure of the society in which his mother and father, and he and his wife and family, lived so comfortably. We must look particularly at the changing relationships between the higher echelons and the lower orders for whose children Sunday schools were established. The eighteenth century was a period of significant transition when the very foundations of the country's institutions were being shaken.

The ordinary, common people, often referred to by their rulers as the lower sort or lowest people, were, until the French Revolution of 1789, regarded as the passive mass of the population; they included all the manual workers – artisans, small shopkeepers, spinners and weavers in the domestic industries, workers in manufactories, farm labourers, fishermen, and paupers. They had no voice in government. As might be expected in a class encompassing such a wide range of occupations, great variations occurred in the living standards of those within it.

The eighteenth century has been described as a 'golden age' and to some communities such an epithet would be appropriate. Where, for instance, employment, food and other necessities of life were readily available and where *noblesse oblige* was the accepted virtue of the day, where landowners and merchant princes, farmers and entrepreneurs cared for their workers and their families, where apprentices enjoyed the same upbringing and sat at the same table as the master craftsman's family, life could be enjoyable. Where poor boys and girls, thanks to the generosity of some school benefactors, received the same assiduous instruction as the pupils whose parents paid fees, and where all the members of the community attended the same church to receive spiritual guidance from a devout, learned, and alert clergyman, amicable social relationships existed. In short where 'ladies and gentlemen' believed in and practised Christian charity, the poor enjoyed a measure of contentment, were respectful and good-natured, and even some social mobility existed. The Revd Gilbert White in his *Natural History of Selborne* published in 1787, said of that village, 'We abound with poor; many of whom are sober and industrious, and live comfortably, in good stone or brick cottages, which are glazed, and have chambers above stairs: mud buildings we have none. Besides the employment from husbandry, the men work in hop gardens, of which we have many; and fell and bark timber. In the spring and summer the women weed the corn; and enjoy a second harvest in September by hop-picking. Formerly, in the dead months, they availed themselves greatly by spinning wool, for making of barragons, a genteel corded stuff, and much in vogue for summer wear . . . The inhabitants' (and this presumably included the poor) 'enjoy a good share of health and longevity; and the parish swarms with children.'[1]

The well-being of communities depended on sympathy between their members and upon each finding happiness in that state of life to which it had pleased God to call him. No rigid class barriers existed. The highest was separated from the lowest by innumerable, easily recognisable gradations in social status. As it was so aptly expressed by one historian, 'The spirit of aristocracy and the spirit of popular rights seemed to have arrived at a perfect harmony, peculiar to the England of that epoch.'[2] Tolerance, and the easy-going nature of society, obviated much resentment and hatred between those of different social position. Only where property was threatened or social disintegration was feared were inflexible attitudes adopted.

Eighteenth century society embodied enormous contrasts, and we must look into, as Raikes himself did, the condition of those at the bottom of the social pyramid. We must also investigate the reasons for the predicament of the poor and why, before Raikes' endeavours, so little was done for their children. Unfortunately, as no official surveys were carried out, we are unable to determine the full extent of the impoverishment suffered, but from accounts by individual observers we can ascertain something of the degree of destitution. One description (published in 1775) of the inadequacy of the living accommodation is included here, and we need to remember, as Raikes' own evidence will show later, that starvation was a not uncommon form of death in his England. 'The shattered hovels which half the poor of this kingdom are obliged to put up with is truly affecting to a heart fraught with humanity,' wrote Nathaniel Kent who, in his work *Hints to Gentlemen of Landed Property*, exhorted landowners to invest money in the building of cottages. 'Those who condescend to visit these miserable tenements, can testify, that neither health or decency, can be preserved in them. The weather frequently penetrates all parts of them; which must occasion illness of various kinds, particularly agues; which more frequently visit the children of cottagers than any others, and early shake their constitutions. And it is shocking that a man, his wife, and half a dozen children should be obliged to lie all in one room together . . . Great towns are destructive both to the morals, and health, and the greatest drains we have; for where many of the lower sort of people crowd together, as in London, Norwich, Birmingham, and other manufacturing towns, they are obliged to put up with bad accommodation, and an unwholesome confined air, which breeds contagious distempers, debilitates their bodies, and shortens their lives.'[3] Since knowledge of such appalling conditions in which subjects of the Crown existed was common, let us try to perceive what kind of monarch, what type of government, and why a national church professing Christianity, remained unmoved by it.

The common people – and very definitely the poor – were, until Raikes' philanthropic endeavours, of little concern to the monarch. The Hanoverian kings who, as we shall see, commanded unwavering loyalty from Raikes' father and then Raikes himself, all exhibited one form of moral turpitude or another. George I (1714–1727), the heavy, slow-minded Elector of Hanover, who at fifty-four had no strong inclination to become King of England, and was 'perhaps the least generally attractive of monarchs', comforted himself with 'blowsy foreign women for his mistresses'.[4] George was constitutionally, and not just in a titular sense, Head of the State, but as he was happier in his palace in Hanover than in his residences in England, he spent half his time there.

George II (1727–1760), son of George I, 'a man greatly superior to his father',[5] though honest, straightforward, businesslike and intrepid, was coarse, vain, selfish, small-minded, and without humour. He despised learning, was avaricious and unfaithful to his wife. He followed precedents set during his father's reign and accepted the gradual erosion of royal power and responsibility. Ministers, whilst being selected by, and legally responsible to, the Crown, found the House of Commons the more exacting master. The Crown was consulted, but the ministers decided: a reversal of the position which had existed prior to the Hanoverian dynasty.

For the common people this entailed little, if any, change in the attitudes or domestic policies of their rulers. The relinquishment of legal rights by the Crown did not give rise to democratic government. A Whig oligarchy from about seventy great landowning families, the heads of which dominated the House of Lords, surrounded the throne. The first two Georges showed preference for Whig ministers, naturally avoiding Tories, some of whom were known to be sympathetic to the Jacobite cause. In the Commons Whig interests were sufficiently strongly represented by cadets and liegemen for the more dignified House of Lords to rest content, allowing itself to function only in an advisory and checking capacity. The predominance of the Whigs in the House of Commons was maintained by what today would be regarded as heinous political corruption – patronage, nepotism, and bribery. Sinecures abounded and politics was a lucrative business.

'Representation' in the House of Commons was absurdly unrepresentative, the seats being very unevenly distributed. Some large towns sent no members at all to the House of Commons, whilst other very small 'pocket' or 'rotten' boroughs, with only a few electors, returned one or even two members. The franchise extended only to 'freeholders' and the support of a voter could be bought. Elections were occasions of noise, feasting and heavy drinking, and not infrequently riot. Sometimes if verbal persuasion and bribery proved ineffective in ensuring the allegiance of a voter, parties resorted to physical intimidation. There was no secret ballot. Whilst vested interests haggled and bartered in the constituencies, leading ministers manipulated elections nationally, browbeating and bribing for support in the House of Commons. Those who took their seats in the Commons via this electoral system were rarely, if ever, deeply committed champions in the cause of the poor.

George III (1760–1820), who became king at the age of twenty-two, was slow, strong-willed and self-confident, brave, good-natured, well-intentioned, religious, and a devoted husband and father. Unfortunately he had been brought up badly by his mother, was bigoted, obstinate, and limited in outlook, and his natural shrewdness was often negated by an inadequate education. Furthermore, popular monarch though he was, and by his personality able to command respect, he nevertheless used bribery extensively to secure power for himself. Although by his actions he did not violate the constitution, his primary aim was the restoration of royal power. This well-liked monarch, who boasted to be 'born and bred a Briton' and to have a passionate love of his country, made many political decisions, but few directed at improving the lot of his most needy subjects. Well-meaning and courageous George III undoubtedly was, but his domination of Parliament boded ill for his country. In March, 1782, when the king's personal government ended, the country had lost its American colonies, virtually an empire, and the national solvency had been greatly endangered.

The common people were not a major concern of central government, Crown, Peers or Commons. One outstanding contrast between Raikes' England and the England of today was the very limited control by the central government of local administration, which was left almost entirely in the hands of the county, the borough, or the parish. The central government accepted no responsibility for those services the statutory provision of which is taken for granted today, such as employment, transport, education, health, or housing. There was no police force and, of course, no social security benefit. In other words eighteenth century central government simply represented the authority which levied taxes and was responsible for the recruitment of men into the army and navy.

Oligarchies of local landowners ruled the provinces. The highest authority responsible to the Crown was the Lord-Lieutenant, usually the greatest landowner in the county and a member of the peerage. He commanded the county militia and, after 1756, appointed the officers of these forces. One of his official responsibilities was to preside over the Quarter Sessions (which he seldom did) and to appoint the clerk of the peace.

A vast amount of power, legal and administrative, rested with the unpaid justices of the peace. Whereas these magistrates in Elizabeth I's reign had been vigilantly watched by the Privy

Council, this direct responsibility to the Crown was discontinued and justices became local despots. Appointed by the Lord Chancellor upon the recommendation of the Lord-Lieutenant, a Minister, or an MP, and having as their primary qualification that of social rank, no conflict of interest existed between them and the local aristocracy: justices of the peace were members of the same class. They received no remuneration. To become a magistrate was regarded as an honour befitting only those with wealth, disinterest (for magistrates swore an oath to treat rich and poor alike), and leisure enough to devote to public service. At the Quarter Sessions magistrates heard both civil and criminal cases, gave orders for the upkeep of roads, bridges, jails, bridewells, workhouses and infirmaries, fixed wages and levied the county rate. In Special Sessions they pronounced on non-jury cases, the licensing of public houses, weights and measures, markets and fairs, and the recruitment of men for army service. Justice was dispensed at the Petty Sessions with two magistrates, or sometimes only one, in attendance.

In his own house a magistrate often dealt summarily with minor offences, imposing fines, committing law-breakers to the stocks, sending them to houses of correction or ordering the whipping of vagrants. Generally speaking, magistrates were well-meaning and beyond corruption, but sole reliance upon their 'common sense justice' – for no legal knowledge was required as a condition of their appointment – led to prejudiced judgements, based on ignorance. And no verdict or decision of a JP could be reversed without an appeal to the judge at the Assize Court, a process well beyond the means of the common labourer.

A similar framework existed in other areas of local government. Incorporated boroughs (municipalities), whilst nominally under the authority of the Lord-Lieutenant, were often autonomous by rights granted under royal charters, and able to enact by-laws applicable within their own boundaries, and appoint municipal justices of the peace to ensure their observance. Throughout the country only the upper strata of society enjoyed political and social dominance. No common man, artisan or labourer, had any representation in Raikes' England.

The absence of legislation to protect the poor or ameliorate their condition illustrates well the lack of concern for them shown by Parliament. Disability and death through drunkenness was the fate of thousands of poor families. Innkeepers' notices offered, 'Drunk for a penny, dead drunk for twopence' and fresh straw for the imbiber to lie on should he or she be too inebriated to stagger home. The appalling increase in the death rate amongst the lowest people at the height of the gin-drinking (1720–1750) did not unduly trouble or arouse great compassion amongst MPs, and the regulation of the sale of gin was achieved only by pressure exerted on Parliament by doctors, magistrates and municipal authorities.

The Act of 1751 which raised the duty on gin and illegalised its sale by chandlers, tobacconists, cobblers, barbers, weavers and the like, is historically significant because it was one of the first pieces of effective legislation for social reform in the eighteenth century. Hard drinking was prevalent in all ranks of society in Raikes' England. The wealthy drank claret, port, sherry, champagne, brandy and porter, whilst the poorer people drank gin and ale. Beer (ale or porter) was the drink of the patriot (see Hogarth's 'Beer Street'), its ingredients, unlike those distilled from grapes, being home produced. It took men of religious conviction to bring about a decline in heavy liquor consumption in the latter part of the century: Wesley and the Methodists, the Evangelicals and, perhaps more importantly, men of the press, like Raikes.

The pursuit of cruel sports was the amusement of members of the gentry and attracted eager followers from the lower orders. These sports included bull and bear baiting, dog-fighting and cock-fighting. The brutality of the worrying of the larger animals by dogs was equalled by the bloody encounters of dogs and cockerels. William Guthrie, author of *A New Geographical, Historical and Commercial Grammar*, published in 1787, regretfully informed us that 'Next to horse-racing and hunting, cock-fighting, to the reproach of the nation, is a favourite diversion among the great, as well as the vulgar. Multitudes of both classes assemble round the pit at one of those matches, and enjoy the pangs of death of the generous animal, every spectator being concerned in a bet, sometimes of high sums.' The barbarous nature of these entertainments, accompanied by reckless wagers, could inculcate only viciousness and irresponsibility in ignorant, uneducated labourers.

In the later decades of the century new economic forces increasingly threatened the stability of the social structure. The revolution in agriculture, attributable to capitalistic farming, beneficial though it was in slowly improving the prosperity and health of the nation generally, adversely affected thousands of small farmers and labourers, depriving them of their livelihood and pauperising them. Efficient farming, it was alleged, required enclosure of land, and many commended the practice. Arthur Young, whose travels included tours through the Southern Counties (1768) and the North of England (1771), writing in 1775, gave it his whole-hearted support. Statesmen, he argued, should lay it down as a maxim, 'that without inclosures there can be no good husbandry: while a country is laid out in open field lands, every good farmer tied down to the husbandry of his slovenly neighbour, it is simply impossible that agriculture should flourish.'[6] The open field system undoubtedly impeded progress in farming, the baulks between strips were wasteful and the practice of using arable fields for grazing cattle in winter prevented the sowing of winter crops. But with enclosure real hardship resulted for the poor who lost their arable strips and use of common pasture. Where the special commission, set up in each case under an Enclosure Act, awarded some land to a peasant, he could not afford the legal requirements of draining and fencing it and therefore had to sell it. Any financial compensation made to him for the loss of a strip was soon spent, in most cases in the ale-house.

The pace of enclosure increased rapidly after 1760. During the whole of the reign of George II the average number of enclosure acts in a year had been seven; between 1760 and 1785 it was forty-seven each year, after which it increased to seventy-eight.[7] Until 1774 a landowner in any part of the country could present a bill to Parliament without even notifying those who were to be affected, and Parliament looked sympathetically upon all bills for enclosure without any consultation of those whose land was to be enclosed. Furthermore to petition against such a bill was not within the ability of illiterate labourers who, in any case, would probably be terrified by even the prospect of dealing with the law. A sentence from one of the few petitions against an enclosure bill in 1774 provides us with some idea of what happened when an enclosure took place. ''Tis . . . computed that there are about sixty families of poor day-labourers in this parish who now find work in the parish; but in case of an inclosure, must all, or the greater part of them, be relieved by the parish.'[8] Enclosure increased the wealth of the rich but brought greater hardship to some of the poor. The labourer lost his strips of arable land, the grazing for his cow and geese on what was formerly common land, and in some areas the right of cutting fuel. The very poor, who had built huts for themselves on the common and squatted there, were moved. Inevitably the enclosing of the land and the engrossing of farms[9] was accompanied by unemployment and the displacement of large numbers of the rural population.

The revolution in industry caused social upheaval and population movement, with all the attendant suffering to the unprotected poor. From about 1760, changes in industrial production, already begun, increased in momentum. The harnessing of water power, the introduction of steam power, the use of coal in working iron, and the concentration of workers in mills started to alter the face of England. Thousands of families, whose traditional skills and occupations in agriculture, particularly, no longer afforded them a livelihood, sought employment in new industries. The relationship between manufacturers and their workers, especially during fluctuations in trade, and the extent to which one industry relied upon another, all added to the complexity of society. In 1750 the ironworks of the Darbys' at Coalbrookdale in Shropshire were alone in using coke firing but, thanks to the efforts of a few men, the iron foundaries of the country were soon to raise the importance in Europe of the whole nation. The invention of the steam engine was decisive in revolutionising industry. Wherever coal, which was in plentiful supply, was found or could be transported easily and cheaply, steam became the economical power for the mills which were then erected in places of geographical advantage. The cotton industry developed in Lancashire, where the climate was favourable for cotton spinning and the port of Liverpool could handle imported raw materials and cotton goods for export.

One further example illustrates the impact these tremendous changes were making upon eighteenth century society. In the mid-eighteenth century the production of woollen and worsted cloth were the leading industries in the country, the cloths being not only an export of growing importance, but the chief source of England's prosperity. Sheep farming preponderated, the flocks being kept mainly for the value of their fleeces: woollen goods

were produced under the domestic system, all the processes of
manufacture being carried on in the houses of the workers. Between household chores, everyone in the home – the housewife
and the older children – could engage in the spinning of wool and
earn a little money. But inevitably, with the invention and introduction of power-driven machinery for the various processes,
production was accelerated, and those using hand-operated
equipment could not compete in the fierce economic market. The
flying shuttle patented by John Kay in 1733 speeded up the work
of the handloom weavers to such an extent that the merchant
clothiers found difficulty in obtaining sufficient yarn to keep them
supplied. Even though poorly paid full employment was found
for those who could use the spinning wheel. Both the shortage of
yarn and the spinning wheel disappeared, however, when Har-
greaves' spinning jenny (1770) and Crompton's spinning mule
(1778) were power driven and employed in mills.

Working conditions in the manufactories throughout the country were atrocious. Unhealthy, ill-ventilated, squalid, sometimes
ramshackle buildings were used, the machinery was dangerous
and lacked adequate safeguards against injury. The hours of work
were intolerably long, sometimes determined by the sheer
exhaustion of the workers. The discipline, to which rural migrants
were unused, was inhuman. Too often foremen, paid according
to the level of production of the workers, were relentless in giving
not a moment for relaxation. Employers deliberately paid low
wages and were eager to employ the cheaper services of women
and children in the dull, repetitive tasks. Promiscuity and immorality was rife in the mills, sometimes with the connivance and
involvement of those in authority. Families worked from early
morning until night for little more than starvation wages. Men
hated the mills as much as they feared prison. Against this barbarity and depravity, this hell, the workers had no redress. Employers, Justices, Members of Parliament and Ministers accepted
no responsibility for the conditions in industry.

1756 saw a change in Government policy towards the cloth
industry. Earlier in the century Parliament dealt sympathetically
with appeals of workers. In 1719 the 'broad and narrow weavers'
of Stroud had successfully petitioned Parliament for justice
against 'tyrannical capitalist clothiers'. Seven years later the
weavers of Somerset and Wiltshire petitioned the Crown against

the 'harshness and fraud' of their employers, and a Committee of
the Privy Council looked into their case, but gave the admonition
that on no account should the workmen combine or attempt redress of grievances themselves, but must seek justice from His
Majesty. In 1728 Gloucestershire weavers appealed to the Justices
of the Peace, who fixed 'a liberal scale of wages for them', and in
1748 Parliament prohibited 'truck', the practice of paying opera-
tives in goods instead of cash. Then in 1756 Parliament brought in
an Act to prevent master clothiers from under-selling and depres-
sing wages by permitting Justices to fix the rates of paying for
piecework, and restrict the number of apprentices being set on for
cheap labour. The Woollen Cloth Weavers' Act caused a dilemma
in Westminster. The clothiers stated that in a fiercely competitive
market they were unable to pay wages fixed by magistrates. The
weavers were supported by the landowners and gentry in claim-
ing, as a legal right, their customary wages. The government pursued a policy of *laissez-faire* and repealed the Act. 'Within a generation the House of Commons exchanged its policy of mediaeval
protection for one of "Administrative Nihilism".'[10]

The great and final authority to which the common man might
turn for justice and solace, the national Church, was, if not wan-
tonly heartless, so damnably caught up in its own corruption as
to neglect its holy trust. The degradation of the Church was such
that the French writer, Charles Montesquieu (1689–1755), averred
during a visit to this country that 'if one talks of religion' in the
higher circles of society, 'everyone laughs'.[11]

Raikes' Church, the Church of England, was regarded by the
ruling aristocracy as a department of state. Almost all the bishops
were nobles, or related to nobles, or former chaplains or tutors to
nobles.[12] George II, very early in his reign, expressed his intention to offer preferment only to gentlemen of quality.[13] The scions
of landowning families who entered the Church did so, not so
much as a calling, but as a profession. They had attended the
same educational institutions as their kinsmen who entered politics or law and were graduates of the same universities. A relative
of the squire was often the local incumbent, tithes, revenues,
endowments and stipends being kept in the family. The father of
Henry Hunt, the famous radical orator, offered to buy Henry a
living where, as a clergyman, he would receive £1,000 a year and
'have nothing else to do for six days out of seven but to hunt,

shoot, and fish by day, and play cards, talk scandal with the old maids of the parish, and win the money of the wives and children of your parish at speculation or Pope Joan . . . All that will be expected of you is to read prayers and preach a sermon, which will cost you threepence once a week, or by a visit to the metropolis you can lay in a stock of manuscript sermons which will last you for the whole of your life.'[14] George Crabbe (1754–1832), the poet, described the life of a clergyman in the Vale of Belvoir thus:

A jovial youth, who thinks his Sunday task
As much as God or man can fairly ask;
The rest he gives to loves or labours light,
To fields the morning, and to feasts the night;
None better skilled the noisy pack to guide,
To urge their chase, to cheer them or to chide;
A sportsman keen, he shoots through half the day,
And, skilled at whist, devotes the nights to play:
Then, while such honours bloom around his head,
Shall he sit sadly by the sick man's bed,
To raise the hope he feels not, or with zeal
To combat fears that e'en the pious feel?

Clerical life proved very attractive to the younger sons of the nobility who entered it in increasing numbers. The ego-ideal of country parsons was to be men of good taste and decorum, having highly elegant diction and a reasonableness in approach productive of deference, respect and sensible conduct amongst their parishioners. Without the white tie the beneficed clergy were indistinguishable from other gentlemen of their acquaintance.

In the matter of preferment to the Episcopate, political obligations, generally speaking, took precedence over spiritual considerations. Government ministers were careful to patronise only those clergy who were completely dependable in their political allegiance and loyalty and who were likely to be assiduous in their service to the government. Inspiring Christian leadership, righteousness, piety, learning, and untiring devotion to the whole Christian family, were attributes of very secondary importance. The political power of bishops was fully appreciated by leaders of the government. A supporting block of twenty-six votes in the House of Lords saved the government embarrassment on more than one occasion. Throughout the country the influence of the bishops was immense. Each bishop was a landed magnate who could command the loyalty and obedience of clergy and churchmen within his see. Through the eyes and ears of his clerics he could be the most knowledgeable government informant and supporter in the province. He could predict, more accurately than most, local reaction to government policy, and via his directives, sermons, and pen, could prove an invaluable political henchman.

Some prelates were learned, hardworking and a credit to their office, often undertaking risky and arduous journeys to visit, bless, confirm, and instruct the faithful of their flock. One or two dared to oppose the government in Parliament, but such diligence in duty and strength of conviction were not typical. No bishop lived frugally and the hospitality which he was expected to extend required a sizable income. So lavish were the entertainments offered by one primate that he was reprimanded by the King for unseemly extravagance. Cornwallis, Archbishop of Canterbury (1768–1783) was renowned for improvements he made to Lambeth Palace, his hospitality and the excellence of his table. George III had occasion to rebuke him severely for his, or more accurately for his wife's extravagance. Mrs Cornwallis was one of the leaders of fashionable society, who was said to eclipse 'everybody by the splendour and magnificence of her equipages and entertainments'.[15]

Besides the corruption of patronage, nepotism and place-hunting, church funds were plundered by pluralism and absenteeism. Pluralism was obviously sensible in small parishes which could not afford singly to support a clergyman, but in the eighteenth century it was accompanied by absenteeism and non-residence. The trade in pluralities resulted in clergymen enjoying the livings from churches they seldom, if ever, visited, the congregations of which were ministered to by ill-paid curates. Clergymen also exploited school endowments, being in receipt of a master's salary when no scholars had been enrolled for years.

In spite of the nadir of their Church there were, however, many devoted Anglican clergy who worked unceasingly, and for the most part unnoticed, to the glory of their religion and men of this calibre readily followed the example set by Raikes. Throughout the country as a whole, all too frequently the needs of the poor were ignored and the cries of the destitute unheeded.

Revelation and salvation for the common man were brought by George Whitefield and John and Charles Wesley. George Whitefield, born and bred in Gloucester, attending both the Crypt and Cathedral (College) Schools there, became the greatest preacher of his age, delivering on average ten sermons a week to congregations sometimes numbering thirty thousand. In 1739 as he preached from the top of a green mound in Kingswood, Bristol, to twenty thousand coal miners, the tears made 'white channels down their blackened cheeks'.[16] Whitefield's thirty-four years' ministry was surpassed only by John Wesley himself, who journeyed a quarter of a million miles preaching on forty thousand occasions following his own maxim, 'Go always, not only to those who want you, but to those who want you most.' Charles Wesley, his younger brother, was both a moving preacher and a great hymn writer, whose inspirational poetry in songs of praise such as 'Jesu, Lover of my soul', 'Hark! the herald-angels sing', and 'Soldiers of Christ, arise' make them favourites today. The expanding population in the growing industrial areas would have received no spiritual guidance but for the labours of the Methodists.

Lastly we must look at the treatment of the children in eighteenth century England, because not only is the civilised nature of society perhaps best ascertained by a study of its concern for its weakest and most defenceless members, but because they became the concern of Raikes. Today public opinion would condemn outright, and authorities would take action against, persons found responsible for exposing children to the risks and cruelty which were commonplace in eighteenth century England.

Army drummer boys, in the front line of battle, were killed and maimed by enemy cannonade and musket fire. At sea young lads were forced to climb the highest masts in fierce winds and high seas, when to slip from the cold, wet rigging meant to crash to death on the ship's deck, or if the ship lurched or heeled over before the wind, to drown in the raging brine. Powder monkeys, boys not in their teens, on men-of-war carried explosive cartridges from the magazine to the gunners. Boys shared the same risks as men.

In industry both sexes suffered terrible usage. Children were employed for the same long hours as adults and paid a trifling amount, sometimes as low as one-sixth of the pay of an adult.

The early mills in Lancashire abounded with child labour. Employers preferred child workers because they learned quickly, were deft, and more easily controlled than their parents. Not only did the children work in the same dreadful conditions as adult employees, but were often bound apprentice for seven years. The discipline and tortures perpetrated upon some of them by mill owners and foremen were horrific. An instance has been recorded of a child having weights placed on his shoulders and being tied almost naked to his machine in winter by his foreman, and of an employer who pinched a child's ears 'until his nails met through the flesh'.[17] The whip and cane were in use all day. Vicious punishments, insufficient sleep, excessive labour, inadequate and bad food, left those who survived the years of drudgery, stunted in growth, mutilated by injuries from men and machines, and deformed physically and mentally. Apprentices left manufactories uncivilised, corrupt, and almost totally ignorant.

Infant mortality among London parish children, and this state of affairs would not be unique to the capital, was shockingly high. A committee of the House of Commons in 1767 examined the registers of several parishes and discovered that 'taking children born in workhouses or parish houses, or received of and under twelve months old, in the year 1763, and following the same into 1764 and 1765, only seven in a hundred appear to have survived this short period.' Further investigation into earlier registers showed that similar mortality rates for young children were known to parish authorities in the years 1754, 1755, 1761 and 1762.[18]

Older pauper children, for whom parish authorities had responsibility, were often dispatched to mills in batches of fifty to a hundred after bargains had been struck between employers who wanted cheap labour and parish authorities anxious to be rid of the burden of keeping the children. Pauper boys were sometimes bound by such an apprenticeship until they reached the age of twenty-four; and in the case of girls twenty-one or until they married. Children of poor parents who were apprenticed to local craftsmen were sometimes nearly as badly off, for they were taught no skills and when trade was bad, they were left to beg for food in the streets. Children had no voice in the decisions made concerning them and their only escape was to run away, back to parents who could not feed them or to a parish which did not want them. The system turned children into vagrants, beggars and thieves.

William Hutton, an apprentice to the Lombe brothers, laboured at their famous mill in Derby. 'I had now,' he wrote, 'to rise at five every morning during seven years, submit to the cane whenever convenient to the master; be the constant companion of the most rude and vulgar of the human race.'[19] No pity was shown because of his age and size. 'Low as the engines were, I was too short to reach them. To remedy this defect, a pair of high pattens were fabricated and lashed to my feet, which I dragged after me till time lengthened my stature. The confinement and labour were no burden, but the severity was intolerable, the marks of which I yet carry and shall carry to the grave.'[20] The treatment of children in the coal mines was as cruel and also more dangerous.

Few ladies or gentlemen were unaware of the suffering of the children of the poor. Every mansion had its chimneys which were swept by a brush held in the hands of a child, and if they missed seeing the poor wretches in their own homes, Jonas Hanway called attention to this devilish practice in 1785 in his *Sentimental History of Chimney Sweepers*. 'There may be (savage nations) who roast their children for food,' declared Hanway, 'but they certainly kill them first; they are not tortured with fire and soot, hunger and thirst, cold and nakedness, and lodgings of the same quality.' The Act of Parliament of 1788 forbade the use of boys under the age of eight in climbing chimneys, and restricted the number of apprentices under one master, but the fact that it proved unworkable was a much the responsibility of those who paid for the sweeps' services as of the sweeps themselves.

There were arguments in abundance to soothe any twinges of conscience experienced by those who could have helped ameliorate the lot of the poor. After all, Christ himself had expressly stated, 'Ye have the poor with you always.' The glorious English Constitution permitted freedom that was the envy of continental countries. Every man, woman, and child was a free agent: free to sell his property and labour for the highest prices he could obtain, and hard though it might be, a free agent must, if he chooses, be free to starve to death. Poverty and riches were regarded as much an act of unfathomable Providence as good health and sickness, fitness and infirmity: the visitation of 'the iniquity of the fathers upon the children unto the third and fourth generation' (Exodus 20.5). Henry Fielding, a magistrate and novelist of humanitarian approach, admitted 'That the Poor are a very great burden and even a nuisance to this kingdom.'[21] With two hundred cargoes of slaves being carried annually in British ships to the 'enrichment' of the nation, a 'slave complex' way of thinking was widespread.

The purpose of this very sketchy social landscape, whilst it is difficult not to engage in value judgements, has been to elucidate Raikes' England. Raikes was himself very conscious of the formidable political, social, economic, and religious structures which have been highlighted. As we shall see, to sublimate and canalise a part of these forces into a means of caring for the children of the poor, whilst at the same time (unlike Pilgrim) ensuring the prosperity of his own family, took the determination of a man like Raikes.

NOTES

[1] Gilbert White, *The Natural History of Selborne* (1833) pp 17–18
[2] G. M. Trevelyan, *History of England* (1943) p 514
[3] Nathaniel Kent, *Hints to Gentlemen of Landed Property* (1775) pp 229–231
[4] Trevelyan, op cit p 531
[5] Ibid p 534
[6] Arthur Young, *Political Arithmetic* (1774) pp 198–199
[7] M. Dorothy George, *England in Transition: Life and Work in the Eighteenth Century* (1953) p 82
[8] *A Petition to the House of Commons against an Inclosure Bill* quoted by M. Dorothy George, *English Social Life in the Eighteenth Century* (1923) p 44
[9] Paul Mantoux, *The Industrial Revolution in the Eighteenth Century* (1961) p 172
[10] Sidney and Beatrice Webb, *The History of Trade Unionism* (1912) p 44
[11] Frank Smith, *A History of English Elementary Education* (1931) p 5
[12] G. M. Trevelyan, *English Social History* (1945) p 360
[13] J. H. Plumb, *England in the Eighteenth Century* (1950) p 42
[14] Robert Huish, *History of Henry Hunt* p 17, quoted by Smith, op cit p 5
[15] J. H. Overton and F. Relton, *A History of the English Church 1714–1800* (1906) p 162
[16] John Richard Green, *A Short History of the English People* (1889) p 737
[17] Mantoux, op cit p 414
[18] *Commons Journals* 1767, xxxi, p 248 quoted by M. Dorothy George, op cit pp 33–34
[19] George, op cit p 61
[20] William Hutton, *The History of Derby* (1791) p 193
[21] H. Fielding, *A Proposal for Making an Effectual Provision etc* (1752) quoted by Dorothy Marshall, *The English Poor in the Eighteenth Century* (1969) p 51

Chapter 2
A FAMILY MAN

Robert Raikes was a family man who knew the importance of family ties. He was no prodigal. It was his respect for his inheritance which destined him to be in a unique position to undertake the endeavours for which he was later acclaimed 'Founder of the Sunday School Movement'. Raikes owed to his family his deep sense of responsibility towards others. The sympathy and understanding he extended to the wider family of his neighbours was engendered by the love he received from his parents; an overspill of the love which he gave to his wife and children.

Mary, his mother, was the daughter of the Revd Richard Drew,[1] of Nailsworth, a village situated thirteen miles south of Gloucester. Considering that Raikes' father, also named Robert Raikes, was a forty-six year old, twice-widowed printer, with surviving daughters of eleven and six, the twenty-one year old Mary appears to have shown exceptional courage in marrying him. (To distinguish between Raikes and his father, the elder Raikes will be referred to as 'Raikes senior'.) A probable explanation for her acceptance of Raikes senior was that he was a most attractive man and that Mary was very much in love with him. They had seven children: a daughter, christened Mary after her mother, and six sons, Robert, Richard who died aged five months, William, Thomas, (another) Richard, and Charles.

Whilst in no sense minimising the importance of his mother's loving care in the development of his personality, it should be recognised that Raikes was greatly indebted to his father and it is worthwhile, therefore, to examine in some detail the life of Raikes senior and note briefly the Raikes family pedigree, of which Mary's first-born son would have had knowledge.

The Raikes family were people of substance. The family name according to one authority was Saxon, but another thought its distant forebears originally came from Denmark. The name was variously spelt amongst its Yorkshire roots – dairy farmers at Kelfield and Eskrigg in Stillingfleet, near York – as Rakys, Rackes and Rakes. At the end of the sixteenth century certain members of the family were attracted to the sea, became sailors and merchants in Kingston-upon-Hull and used the spelling Raikes. A Robert Raikes became a free burgess of Hull in 1599 and, in 1616, a Warden of Trinity House, the special corporation instituted in Hull for the settlement of disputes between shipowners and sailors and responsible for decisions regarding the administration of numerous charities for seamen. During the seventeenth century several members of the Raikes family became Brethren and Wardens of Trinity House.

The line of descent to Robert Raikes of Gloucester can be traced from Richard Raikes, a merchant who settled in Hull in 1610. Richard had five sons and eight daughters. Only two sons, Joshua and Richard, survived infancy. The third daughter, Esther, married twice; her second husband was a William Wilberforce from whom was descended the great evangelical philanthropist and founder of the Anti-Slavery Society, William Wilberforce. Richard, Esther's brother, studied at Emmanuel College, Cambridge, where a degree of Master of Arts was conferred upon him. Eventually he entered the Church and became Curate of Beeford, Yorkshire, and afterwards Vicar of Hessle, near Hull. He died in 1671 and was survived by three sons and three daughters.

Timothy, the eldest son of this Revd Richard Raikes, was the father of Raikes senior. Timothy entered St John's College, Cambridge in 1667, and like his father entered the Church obtaining preferment as Vicar of Tickhill in 1674, after which in 1689 he became Vicar of Hessle, his late father's parish. Timothy married Sarah Partridge of Gloucester and had thirteen children, of whom four sons and three daughters survived childhood.

Raikes senior, Timothy's eldest surviving child, for unaccountable reasons entered the printing trade and became a pioneer of the newspaper industry. He was born in 1689 and baptised at Hessle on 22 April, 1690. On 1 October, 1705, at the age of sixteen, he was bound apprentice to one John Barker of Lambeth Hill, London, and from then onwards experienced the ups and downs of life: he knew the joys of fulfilment, but suffered the stresses of business and the sorrow of bereavements. In 1718 he appears to have been in the employ of Thomas Gent of York and to have learnt his trade sufficiently well to be recommended by this 'eminent printer' for a post with a Mr Hasbert of Norwich. If

Raikes senior did take the job with Hasbert he could not have stayed with him long as in the same year he set up his own press in St Ives, Huntingdonshire, where he showed his interest in the newspaper business by printing his first weekly, priced three halfpence, and entitled the *St Ives Post Boy; or, The Loyal Packet*. Raikes senior's press was not the first in St Ives for a J. Fisher in 1716 had printed a paper, *St Ives Post* and it seems likely that Raikes senior purchased Fisher's business. Before the end of 1719 Raikes senior replaced this earlier paper with the *St Ives Mercury*. About this time he was on friendly terms with William Dicey of Northampton, a young man of similar employment and interest: the two became partners in a weekly newspaper, the *Northampton Mercury or Morning Post*, which first appeared on 2 May, 1720. Dicey seems to have been the practical manager, Raikes senior taking control of the literary side of the enterprise. The business soon expanded and the partners set up a printing office in Gloucester.

Gloucestershire held a special attraction for Raikes senior, for not only had his mother, Sarah Raikes, née Partridge, lived in the county, but he himself had become engaged to Sarah the daughter of John and Abergale Niblett of Lechlade, a village thirteen miles east of Cirencester and thirty miles from Gloucester.[2] Visits to Lechlade probably made Raikes senior aware of the opportunities open to a printer in Gloucester. The idea of launching a newspaper there could have been reinforced by the closing down of the small weekly newspaper, the *Cirencester Post*, one of the earliest newspapers in the country to be printed. Raikes senior probably came to Gloucester alone, setting up a printing office in Northgate Street and leaving Dicey to manage the business in Northampton.

Fortune smiled on Raikes senior. He married Sarah Niblett on 25 February, 1722, and on 10 March, 1722, he put up a notice: 'At the Printing Office against the "Swan Inn" in Gloucester will be shortly published Weekly a Newspaper entitled the "Gloucester Journal"; which will contain not only the most authentic Foreign and Domestick News, but also the price of Corn, Goods, &c., at Bear Key in London, and all Trading Cities and Market Towns 50 miles herewith', and on 9 April, 1722 the first edition of the *Gloucester Journal* came off the press. A daughter was born of his marriage to Sarah and christened after her mother. In less than a year, however, his wife died and he found himself a widower at the age of thirty-four, but he did not stay a widower for long. About a year after the death of Sarah he married again. His second wife, Anne, was the sister of William Mond, MD, of Walthamstow, Essex. The couple made their home in Gloucester, near the printing business in the parish of St Mary de Crypt. Raikes senior's second marriage, like his first, was ill-fated. A son, Robert, was born on 18 October, 1726, but lived only three weeks. Three years later on 18 March, 1729, Anne had a daughter, Elizabeth, and on 10 September, 1731, a second daughter Martha. Martha lived only until the following April, and it was three years to the day after the birth of Martha, that Anne herself was buried.

In his business enterprises, as a printer, newspaper proprietor, and vendor of 'quack' medicines, Raikes senior was successful, but these interests did not leave him free from worry. His business partnership with William Dicey had been dissolved in 1725, Dicey retaining the Northampton business, Raikes senior taking over the Gloucester concerns.[3] Being an enterprising newspaperman he had collaborated with Edward Cave, the founder and editor of the *Gentleman's Magazine* in providing his readers with news of the proceedings of the House of Commons and had published some extracts from the Minutes of the House supplied by Cave. As such reporting at the time was strictly forbidden both Cave and Raikes senior were summoned to be punished for having committed a breach of the privileges of Parliament. On 26 March, 1728, 'Robert Raikes in the custody of the Sergeant at Arms . . . was brought to the Bar where he (and Cave) upon (their) knees received a reprimand from Mr Speaker.' The offenders acknowledged their error and on payment of fines were released.[4]

Adverse criticism of his patriotism and loyalty to the Constitution followed the summons to London, to such an extent that he felt the need to vindicate himself thus in the next edition of the *Gloucester Journal*: 'Since the Printer hereof hath been under the Displeasure of the House, it hath been industriously and maliciously insinuated, that it is for Printing against the Government; which is a false and scandalous Aspersion.'[5]

A second charge for a similar offence was brought against Raikes the next year and he was again ordered to appear at the Bar of the House of Commons. This time, however, he did not attend, but sent an apology in which he explained that he was suffering from a fever and was therefore unfit to travel and that the offending passages had been published without his knowledge and contrary to his specific orders. In view of the circumstances the House showed leniency and 'discharged Raikes from attendance'. Raikes senior was no doubt especially careful not to offend a third time, because in its determination to keep its proceedings secret the House passed a resolution to the effect that anyone who printed in a newspaper 'any account or minutes of the debates or other proceedings of this House, or of any committee thereof' would be severely punished.[6]

In spite of these misdemeanours and the allegations against him, Raikes senior appears to have been held in some regard in his own parish where, in the same year of 1729 in which he committed his second offence, he was elected Overseer of St Mary de Crypt.

Raikes senior proved himself to be a man of enterprise, ability, and perseverance, who became widely known as 'the printer of Gloucester'. Under his proprietorship and editorship the *Gloucester Journal* met a need and its circulation throughout Gloucestershire and the neighbouring counties increased. Although the original issues were only $12\frac{1}{4}$ by $7\frac{3}{4}$ inches in size they each contained twelve columns of summaries; foreign and home news, often extracts from London papers, reports on crimes, trials, and executions, mishaps and sporting events and sundry advertisements, such as property for rent, auction sales, new books, and, of course, 'quack' medicines. Raikes senior, particularly as his family responsibilities increased, strove to improve his paper and to attract new readers by several times altering the shape of the headlines and rearranging the layout and in August, 1742 he enlarged the sheets to 16 by $10\frac{1}{2}$ inches. Roland Austin's conclusions are apt and pertinent: 'Throughout the whole period of his ownership the "Gloucester Journal" displays a vigour and intelligence of direction which proves Raikes to have been no ordinary journalist. The various changes effected in the paper, and his addresses to his subscribers, indicate the pride and interest which he bestowed upon it.'[7]

The sideline, the sale of 'quack' medicines, engaged in by both Dicey and Raikes senior, was profitable; sufficiently profitable to be continued by Raikes, father and son, despite its dubious respectability and the ethical considerations in view of the impossible claims made by those advertising their preparations. Although the insertion of advertisements for remedies which would cure like magic the ailments of members of all classes of society was not unusual in eighteenth century newspapers, it is perhaps surprising to read in the columns of the *Gloucester Journal*, published during the time when Raikes (junior) was in full vigour and control, and without the safeguard of a heading 'Advertisement', that 'Maredant's Drops' would eradicate (as well as many other ills) 'Leprosy', and that 'Chinese Lotion' which 'may be had in quart Moulded Bottles of 5s each by asking Mr Raikes at the Printing Office' would 'absolutely prevent Venereal Infection, or the Communication of the disease at any Stage'; and that 'Leake's justly famous pill', sold 'in boxes of 2s 6d each at the Printing Office in Gloucester' was 'pronounced to be cure for Venereal Disease, the Scurvy and Rheumatism'.[8] Business was business.

Whether from moneys left to him by his first wife, or from the profits of his business, the founder of the *Gloucester Journal* was wealthy enough in a few years to invest in property. When Henry Wagstaffe, county sheriff in 1708, and a member of a well-to-do Gloucester family, died in 1725, he left, according to his will, debts which his widow, Margaret, was unable to settle. Mortgages on the Wagstaffe property in Gore Lane, Gloucester, were taken over by Raikes senior in 1728 and foreclosed in 1731–2. In 1732 he undertook the tenancy of the Wagstaffe residence, Ladybellegate House, a very fine property in Longsmith Street, Gloucester, and later, in 1735, acquired all the property owned or leased by Margaret Wagstaffe.

Whatever the depth of his sorrow over the loss of his second wife, Raikes senior did not let his bereavement eclipse his life unduly because at the age of 46, as already mentioned, he had won the heart of Mary Drew, a young lady twenty-five years his junior. In September, 1736, Raikes (junior), their eldest son, was born[9] and baptised Robert in the Church of St Mary de Crypt on 24 September, 1736.

In 1743 Raikes senior moved his printing office to Blackfriars, off Southgate Street, and he and his family took up residence in a 'Mr Cockerell's House in the Friers' near to his printing office. The advertisement in the *Gloucester Journal* 8 March, 1743, gives an interesting description of the property he vacated: 'To be Lett at Midsummer next, The House wherein R. Raikes, the Printer, now lives, having the following Conveniences, viz. four good Cellars, a Landry, and a good Brew-House with a Rain-Water Cistern that will hold near Sixty Hogsheads, and a good Spring Water Pump.'

Of Raikes' early childhood little is known, but his mother, a clergyman's daughter, would have been educated as well as most middle class girls at the time and would bring her children up with such generosity, humility, refinement and taste as would be acceptable to her own social group. The nature and extent of Raikes' secular schooling is uncertain, except that his youngest daughter, at the age of eighty-four, could recall that her father 'wrote French fluently and was a first rate geographer'.[10] It is very probable that he was sent to St Mary de Crypt School, the church and the school being adjacent buildings and Raikes senior's house only a short distance away. Raikes' parents both attended St Mary de Crypt Church and their seven children were all christened there, as the memorial tablet and baptismal register testify. Attendance at the Crypt, the ancient grammar school founded in 1539, would have offered acceptable pedagogy and social standing for the son of a printer. In 1751 at the age of fourteen Raikes was enrolled as a scholar at the College (Cathedral) School, but no date of leaving is known. The transfer would not be remarkable, the College School being regarded as a higher grade grammar school than the ancient grammar school, the Crypt, and therefore a suitable school at which to extend Raikes' education.

However short his schooling there, Raikes, to judge from the obituary he wrote, appears to have formed a high regard for his headmaster and appreciated the tuition he received: 'On Tuesday last were interred at the church of St Mary de Crypt, in this city, the remains of the Rev. Mr Sparks . . . This gentleman, about eight years ago, resigned the Upper Mastership of the College (Cathedral) School, in this city; which important office he had discharged with great and deserved credit for upwards of 30 years. His goodness of heart, and genuine erudition, conciliated the love and respect of his scholars; and all must regard his memory with gratitude, who consider, that, under his tuition, were formed many, who have been, and still are, the shining ornaments of this county.'[11]

Whatever his formal education Raikes' parents had a very strong formative influence on his life and character and he grew up to be a religious man and a constant communicant at St Mary de Crypt Church.

The certain intention that Raikes should enter his father's business was affirmed by the Revd Samuel Glasse, one of Raikes' friends in later life, in a pamphlet he wrote in 1788. 'At a proper time of life he was initiated into the employment of his father, which was not limited to the business of a journalist, but extended itself to other branches of typography.'[12] Raikes senior was obviously determined that his eldest son should have the benefit of a full 'Apprenticeship' in his business before undertaking responsibility for the control and running of it. From both his father and his mother Raikes probably learned his vocational expertise. No doubt much of his business acumen, ability as an editor, and skill as a printer, are attributable to his father's example and teaching, because we know that he was serving his 'apprenticeship' in 1755 and freed on 4 October, 1757. He had but few years' experience in business with his father.

On 7 September, 1757 Raikes senior died at the age of sixty-eight having made comfortable provision for his wife and children. His will shows his especial concern for the 'Education of his five younger children'. He entreated the executors to apply 'their utmost care respectively in and about the Morals and Education of them'. His business he left to his eldest son, Robert, and the 'heirs of his Body lawfully to be begotten'.

His parents had obviously agreed that whilst their eldest son should eventually inherit the business he must first pursue his father's 'Trade and business of a Printer and Stationer', and that in the event of his father's decease, 'in order to preserve the same trade and business for him' Mary, his mother, should 'to the utmost of her power preserve and carry on the said trade for her own benefit and maintain (Robert) . . . until he shall be out of his apprenticeship'. At such time Mary was then to take him into partnership 'and permit him to have equal profit with her'. When he reached the age of twenty-five she was then to 'entirely relinquish and turn over the said trade to him' in its entirety 'for his own proper use and benefit'.

Almost immediately after his father's decease Raikes, who in all probability had not quite reached his twenty-first birthday, was involved in the running of the business. He proved equal to the demands made by the thriving newspaper and printing business and the next year showed enterprise in moving his printing office from Blackfriars to more imposing premises in Southgate Street, Gloucester. The passage in the *Gloucester Journal* of 22 August, 1758 announcing the move gives us a clear idea of the goodwill both Raikes, father and son, enjoyed from their subscribers. 'R. Raikes Begs leave to acquaint the Publick that he has Removed his Printing Office from Black-Fryars to the House of Mr. William Coles, Ironmonger, lately lived in Southgate Street. He gladly embraces this opportunity of expressing his grateful Acknowledgements to all his friends for the kind Encouragement with which they have favoured him since his Father's Death: He further hopes, that they will still continue the same Benevolence towards him, and augment, by Addition of future Obligations, the Debt which they have already laid upon his Gratitude; assuring them that the whole Bent of his Endeavours shall be, to repay Regard with Service, and to Add to the Happiness of enjoying their kindness the Credit of deserving it.' What a salesman! Under his management the business continued to thrive and the family prospered.

As head of the family Raikes saw his sister and brothers educated and well placed.[13] His sister married Francis Newberry, Esq, of Addiscombe, Surrey and Heathfield Park, Sussex, at St James's, Bath, on 29 May, 1770. His younger brothers William, Thomas, and Charles all went into business in London, no doubt encouraged by their uncle, Timothy Raikes, who was a merchant of some importance in the capital and who had extensive business connections in Russia. William eventually became a Director of the South Sea Company and married Martha Pelly, the daughter of a Governor of the Bank of England.

Thomas achieved great heights. He was renowned in London circles of commerce for his wealth and probity. In 1797 he became a Governor of the Bank of England and counted Pitt and Wilberforce (who was a distant relative) among his friends.

Richard, Raikes' third brother, seven years his junior, was attending the College School, Gloucester, when his father died. He was later able to complete his education at St John's College, Cambridge, after which he entered the Church. He returned to Gloucester accepting an appointment as tutor to the daughters of

Lady Guise, and in 1793 was appointed to the Perpetual Curacy of Maisemore, a village four miles north-west of the city. Charles, Raikes' youngest brother and eight years his junior, also became a merchant in London.

Raikes, himself, did not marry until he was thirty-one, when he chose Anne, only daughter of Thomas Trigge of Newnham, near Gloucester, whose brothers became General Sir Thomas Trigge, KCB, and Rear Admiral John Trigge. The wedding was solemnised on 23 December, 1767, in St James' Church, Piccadilly. At the time of her marriage Anne was staying with her mother, Mrs Napier, in Great Pulteney Street, Golden Square, W.

Raikes and his bride returned to Gloucester to make their home in Ladybellegate House. They had ten children. Their first two children died young: Anne, the eldest daughter, in infancy and a son, Robert Powell, when eleven years old. They then had six daughters before a male heir, Robert Napier, was born. Their youngest child, another son, was christened William Henley.

Raikes was an affectionate husband and father and frequently spoke of his 'dear wife' and his 'six excellent daughters and two lovely sons'. He and his wife were attentive to their children's education and delighted in their social successes. The Gloucester branch of the family, like all the Raikeses, were outgoing. Raikes kept the household of a gentleman of the period and entertained 'the best company'. Many distinguished persons coming to Gloucester visited the Lord Bishop at the Palace, the Mayor and then Raikes. James Whitehead, Raikes' office boy, who often helped the footman, recalled clearly that 'Mrs Raikes was never happy unless her house was full of company'.[14] A further indication of Raikes' love of company is to be found in Fanny Burney's account of her visit in 1788: 'They all received us with open arms. They seem to live with great hospitality, plenty, and good cheer. They gave us a grand breakfast and then did the honours of their city.' Fanny Burney's opinions, however, would seem not always to be too reliable as, although she found Mrs Raikes to be 'a quiet, unpretending woman', she described her daughters as 'common sort of country misses'[15] which judgement does not seem to be borne out by the marriages they eventually made.

Their eldest daughter, also named Anne, born 17 September, 1771, married Admiral Sir Thomas Boulden Thompson, Bart, when he was Captain Sir Thomas, RN, on 25 February, 1799.

Mary, the second daughter, born 17 September, 1773, married Henry Garrett, RN, (later promoted Admiral Garrett) on 5 November, 1796. Twins, Albinia and Eleanor, were born on 12 September, 1775. Albinia married John Birch, Esq, Charlotte Street, Bloomsbury Square, Lieut-Colonel of the Royal Westminster Volunteers on 14 May, 1799, and Eleanor married Daniel Garrett, Esq, of Gower Street, Bedford Square on 20 June, 1797. Charlotte, the fifth daughter, born 27 November, 1776, married Commander William Stanley Clarke, a Director of the East India Company, on 1 May, 1798, and the youngest daughter, Caroline, born 28 February, 1779, married Captain James Weller, 23 Regiment of Light Dragoons (afterwards General Weller Ladbroke) in 1803. Obviously gentlemen of rank and position were pleased to come into and be married from Raikes' home.

Both the Raikes' boys became well established professionally. The elder, Robert Napier, born 3 November, 1783, graduated B A at Oriel College, Oxford, and took holy orders. In September, 1810 he married Caroline, daughter of the Very Revd John Probyn of Longhope and Newland, Gloucestershire, and Dean of Llandaff, and in 1812 became Rector of Hillesden and Drayton, Norfolk, and later Rector of Longhope. William Henley, born 18 April, 1785, entered the Coldstream Guards, attaining the rank of Colonel. He married Louisa, youngest daughter of Henry Boulton, Esq, of Givons Grove, Leatherhead.

As is already evident, the Raikes family was, for the times, unexceptional in its class consciousness, yet this was tempered with charitableness. James Whitehead, already quoted, made perspicacious remarks about his mistress, Mrs Raikes, 'She was very "pettish" but very good, and had her own way, but she kept the maids a long time, and she was very charitable. We all knew she was a lady – an admiral's sister.'[16]

Raikes took pride in his family and the family life widened rather than restricted his horizons. The diversity of the callings of the Raikeses and their partners in marriage; their education, width of travel and experience, and positions of responsibility, would militate against narrow prejudice.

Raikes, the devoted son, was an equally kind, loving husband and father. His love for Anne, his wife, is clearly revealed in his worry about her when she was unwell in 1790. In an apology for neglecting a business matter he wrote: 'I have been greatly distressed by the indisposition of my wife, whom I have been obliged to attend into the country for the benefit of her health.'[17] Caroline, Raikes' youngest daughter, in 1862 at the age of 84, referred to her 'dearest' and 'beloved father' as a most affectionate husband and father.

The glimpses into the Raikes' home through the eyes of his servants show Mrs Raikes (his wife) to be 'a very good, pious woman' and the family living 'affectionately together'.[18] Raikes, himself, was portrayed as a 'nice, good looking man ',[19] very sociable and well spoken: a man 'regular in his habits'. He is said to have 'kept a good table' and to have enjoyed his after-dinner wine.[20] Raikes kept a man-servant and three maid-servants and was considered by one to be 'a good, liberal master' who 'paid good wages' and 'kept his servants a good while' and by another 'a kind hearted sort of man'.[21] He appears not to have entered into conversations on religious subjects with his servants and to have held family prayers only on Sundays 'and then his servants always attended them'.[22]

What his family thought of his image outside the home is unrecorded, but he was 'considered by some a very ostentatious sort of man' and represented as 'a very buckish sort of person when he was young' with 'always a great deal of style about him'.[23] Fanny Burney's first, and only, impression of Raikes might have been shared by others, 'Mr. Raikes', she wrote after her visit to Gloucester in 1788, 'is not a man that without a previous disposition towards approbation I should greatly have admired. He is somewhat too flourishing, somewhat too forward, somewhat too voluable; but he is witty, benevolent, good natured, and good hearted, and therefore the overflowing of successful spirits and delighted vanity must meet with some allowance.'[24] The curate of his own church, St Mary de Crypt, who was supposed to have known him well, said of him in 1831: 'An excessive vanity was a prominent feature in Mr Raikes's character.'[25]

Of fair complexion, medium height, 'somewhat portly' or 'comfortably stout', Raikes walked with a swagger.[26] He wore extravagant, elaborate, expensive, fashionable attire: 'a dark blue or claret coat and white, buff, or fancy waistcoat with silver-gilt buttons, and not too elaborate cambric frill and cuffs'; nankeen (cloth in winter) breeches, white stocking and buckles on his shoes. He had a brown wig, with two rows of curls, and a three cornered hat which could be carried under the arm. Raikes took snuff, carrying with him a horn box, but for dress occasions he had a massive gold box and practised the habit 'with elegance'.[27]

Raikes' ostentation and pompousness seem to have been deliberate and he was almost certain to have been aware that 'when he walked he drew attention to himself',[28] because his mannerisms were probably a manifestation of his authoritarian philosophy. Prosperity and confidence reflect security and efficiency. A stylish, prosperous appearance is good for business. Raikes was a successful business man.

Raikes was wealthy. Viewed from the standpoint of the seven classes into which Daniel Defoe divided the population in the early eighteenth century,[29] Raikes senior maintained his family as the middle sort, who lived well, whilst his sons Robert, William, and Thomas elevated their respective households to the rich, who lived plentifully.[30] Generosity within the family was noticeable, as instanced in the promotion of the careers of Raikes' brothers, William, Thomas and Charles, by their uncle, and it is worth noting that Raikes did not forget in his opulence even the poor of his grandfather's parish, as can be seen in an acknowledgement in Hessle Church: 'Robert Raikes of the City of Gloucester gave £100 which is lent to the overseers of the poor at 5 p.c. and secured in the Parish Poor House.'

Raikes had no illusions about the advantages of being wealthy. Financial acquisitions were vitally important to the security and well-being of his family. Health, strength, education, social acceptance, even graciousness and generosity depended on it. In his profession he was daily reminded of the precariousness of existence in eighteenth century England without it. He knew full well the misery and dangers which confronted the poor.

Raikes was a homely man, who loved his family. Cheerful, shrewd, able, methodical, he was equal to the demands of his profession. He ran a printing business and lucrative sidelines, as well as editing the most important newspaper in the West Midlands, perhaps the most important in the West Country.

He was a devout churchman, attending not only St Mary de Crypt Church, but also services in the Cathedral, often with a business associate, Mr James Wood, a banker. Raikes cannot, with accuracy, be described as an Evangelical, in the eighteenth century interpretation of the word. He was a religious man, but for him there was not the same conviction as for Wesley and Whitefield 'that nothing except religion mattered'.[31] He might have been said to have lived for his faith, but not to the extent of forsaking the world. Raikes was a man of the world. Overall, he appears to have been a kindly, benevolent man, who 'liked to have children about him', had a 'nice way about him with them' and was very fond of them.[32]

Certain conclusions become evident from a study of Raikes' life. The love he enjoyed within his own home as a boy and its influence upon his own personality is attributable to his mother. He learned from his father the importance of undertaking useful work and the satisfaction to be derived from making his contribution to the common weal. He understood happiness to be the consequence of sensible living and his philanthropic endeavours expressed his own practical Christianity.

NOTES

[1] Probably vicar of the church in Horsley; J. H. Harris (editor), *Robert Raikes: The Man and his Work* p 255

[2] John Niblett was in business as a 'carrier'. Sarah Raikes (née Niblett) appears to have owned property.

[3] 20 September, 1725 was the last issue of the *Gloucester Journal* bearing the names of both Dicey and Raikes.

[4] The report appeared on page 1 of the *Gloucester Journal*, 12 March, 1728 and consisted of thirty lines on the State of the National Debt. The paragraph cost Raikes £40

[5] *Gloucester Journal*, 30 March, 1728

[6] Harris, op cit p 333

[7] Roland Austin, *Robert Raikes, the Elder, and the Gloucester Journal* (1915) p 21

[8] *Gloucester Journal* 31 August, 1778; 9 November, 1778; 22 February, 1779

[9] W. F. Lloyd, *Sketch of the Life of Robert Raikes and of the History of Sunday Schools* (1826) p 7. The *Dictionary of National Biography* says Raikes was born 14 September 1735. This is a common error. In the Raikes family pedigree, 'corrected to January 25th, 1897' no date for birth is given. The entry is 'b. at Gloucester, bapt. at St. Mary de Crypt, 24 Sep. 1736'. The date 14 September 1735 is apocryphal, and the error probably originated in an article by Samuel Glasse in the *Gentleman's Magazine* in 1788. It was perpetuated in *Fosbroke's History of Gloucester* 1819, and subsequent publications.

[10] Harris, op cit p 209 (Raikes' youngest daughter's letter).

[11] *Gloucester Journal* 2 May, 1785

[12] *Gentleman's Magazine* 1788 Vol LVIII(i) p 12

[13] Sarah, Raikes' stepsister by his father's first marriage, died in February, 1739. Elizabeth, his stepsister by his father's second marriage, married Thomas Jeffries of London, 16 May, 1751.

[14] Harris, op cit p 187

[15] M. D'Arblay, *Diary* 19 July, 1788 quoted by Alfred Gregory, *Robert Raikes: Journalist and Philanthropist* (1880) p 167

[16] Harris, op cit p 187

[17] Raikes, *Letter* 12 July, 1790 also 15 January, 1793

[18] William Redding, indoor servant to Raikes (1807) quoted Harris, op cit p 191

[19] William Whitehead, ibid p 188

[20] William Redding, ibid pp 190–191

[21] William Whitehead, ibid p 188

[22] William Redding, ibid p 190

[23] Miss Priscilla Kirby, ibid pp 27–28

[24] Gregory, op cit p 167

[25] Arthur B. Evans, *Gentleman's Magazine* October 1831 p 295

[26] Harris, op cit pp 48, 49

[27] Ibid

[28] Ibid p 49

[29] *Review* 25 June, 1709.
 Defoe's divisions:
 1 The great, who live profusely.
 2 The rich, who live very plentifully.
 3 The middle sort, who live well.
 4 The working trades, who labour hard but feel no want.
 5 The country people, farmers, etc, who fare indifferently.
 6 The poor, that fare hard.
 7 The miserable, that really pinch and suffer want.

[30] According to an Indenture in the possession of the National Christian Education Council, a marriage settlement of £1,000 was made by Raikes on his daughter Eleanor.

[31] Paul Sangster, *Pity My Simplicity* (1963) p 18

[32] James Whitehead, quoted Harris, op cit p 187, 188

Chapter 3

EDITOR AND PRISON VISITOR

As the editor of the *Gloucester Journal*, one of the 'two greatest of all provincial papers'[1] in the country, Raikes was confronted with the whole spectrum of human existence: monarch and beggar, plenty and starvation, learning and ignorance, wisdom and stupidity, benevolence and miserliness, gentleness and viciousness, forgiveness and mercilessness. By the very nature of his profession he was continually dealing with information about the unusual and extreme, particularly with conflict and disorder, which were the consequence of complex social problems.

In trying to trace the influences upon Raikes which put him in a unique position to become the central figure in the Sunday School Movement, a few examples have been selected from the *Gloucester Journals* 1756–57. This period covered the last year of Raikes' apprenticeship and the extracts illustrate how well the young editor had observed his father's expertise. Both Raikeses, father and son, were not simply the proprietors and editors of the newspaper, they were also sub-editors, reporters, writers of leading articles, and proof-readers, besides taking responsibility for printing and distribution. Of course they employed skilled craftsmen, compositors and printers who, on occasion when libellous material had been printed, could be blamed for the 'mistake' or 'error of judgement'.

The content of the *Gloucester Journal*, in accordance with common demand of readers of the provincial newspapers, was chiefly concerned with international and national news obtained from the London papers. The remaining columns were filled with material selected much more at the discretion of the editors; the policy by which such items would be selected was elucidated by Raikes senior during the third year of its establishment. He wrote, 'A newspaper is generally like a Coffee-House, wherein everyone expects to have his Intelligence taken notice of; for which Reason (in Condescention to our Correspondents) we generally have a favourable Opinion of what is transmitted to us, believeing that

45

every one that sends us any Thing, is desirous it should be communicated to the Public; by which means we are sometimes liable
to be impos'd upon, notwithstanding we endeavour to publish
Nothing but what is Genuine.'[2]

Raikes, in the last edition of the *Gloucester Journal* in which his
father's name appeared as the printer, declared his firm intention
to defend the same freedom that his father had enjoyed, to
include that which could be judged 'genuine' and of public interest. In reporting the consequences of the Stamp Act of 1757,
whereby the price of the newspaper and the cost of advertising
was increased, he took the opportunity to drive home to his readers the importance of maintaining a 'free press'. 'I will not pre-
sume to say,' wrote Raikes, circumspectly in reference to the Act,
but nevertheless putting suspicion of a possible threat to 'freedom' in the mind of his reader, 'that this Proceeding of the Legislature has its Rise in a Design to subvert the Liberty of the PRESS,
in which every other Liberty of an Englishman in some Measure
depends; or to suppress that Kind of Intelligence to which all my
Countrymen have a Right, and an Interest, to know. However
this be, it is at present in the Power of my Readers to defeat any
Attempt of this Kind, by continuing to take the GLOUCESTER
JOURNAL at the small Advance above mentioned; whereby they
will encourage me to continue its Publication (in which my Father
has happily succeeded to their Satisfaction for upwards Thirty
Years) and will increase the Obligation I now lie under, to use my
utmost Endeavours to render it as useful and entertaining as the
Nature of the Undertaking will permit.'[3]

An example of the elder Raikes' diplomacy can be found in the
reporting of events during the dispute between the clothiers and
broadcloth weavers in 1756, to which reference has already been
made.[4] Protesting about the poor pay received for their work, the
general body of broadcloth weavers made application to the Court
at the 'General Sessions of Peace of (the) County' to determine
the 'price of weaving' ie, wages to be paid. The magistrates,
although 'thoroughly disposed to give them (the weavers) all the
relief to which it was empowered' under an Act of Parliament
passed the previous year, found it impossible to make such a
judgement because of 'the very great variety of sorts of Broadcloth' being produced, and in consequence of its inability to pro-
ceed further, the Court requested both the clothiers and weavers

to prove themselves men of 'Honesty' and 'integrity' and settle the matter between themselves. As the manufacture of cloth was a leading major industry in the country it would have been reasonable to assume that the rights and wrongs involved would have been a subject of wide interest, and by printing the arguments Raikes could have profitably extended his readership. However, he refused to take the risk of further arousing already inflamed passions knowing that unlawful actions taken by workers who felt unjustly treated could lead them to the gallows. Instead, whatever Raikes' own predilections in respect of the arguments proffered, the court findings were reported fully and soberly in the *Gloucester Journal* on 12 October, 1756, with an additional column from Raikes supporting the recommendations of the Court and pointing out the dangers which lay in 'Oppression' by the clothiers and 'Redress' by unlawful means on the part of the weavers. Having done this he would publish correspondence from neither party. The outcome, already mentioned, was that Parliament decided upon a policy of *laissez-faire* and later repealed the Act.

Raikes senior, on the other hand, not only published details of charitable enterprises in his paper, but he used his presses to print matter or material to be sold for charity. One such example, which his son was to emulate many times, was recorded in the *Gloucester Journal*, 27 July, 1756. 'Gloucester. On Thursday last was paid to the Secretary of the Infirmary by Mr. Raikes, £27 being a further Benefaction to that Charity of the Hon. & Rev. Mr. Talbot's and whole Profit arising from the Publication of his Sermon preached in August last at the Opening of the Infirmary.'

Raikes senior also constantly focused public attention on those in distress during the serious food shortage of 1756–57. The editions of the *Gloucester Journal* for the autumn, winter and spring of 1756–57 contain many examples of Christian charity extended to the poor. These are of particular interest because not only do they appear to reflect the attitude of Raikes senior towards the poor, but also because a decade later his son's approach to the reporting of an even more serious food crisis was in many ways the same.

The bad harvest in 1756 caused scarcity and a consequent steep rise in the cost of wheat and therefore the price of bread. Wages, if they rose at all, did not keep up with prices and half-starved people rioted in the markets up and down the country. In

Gloucestershire colliers from the Forest of Dean plundered wheat barges on the River Severn and even 'pulled down Parrey's Mills, near Ross', with the result that some of the rioters were arrested and taken to Gloucester gaol. At Chepstow, a border town on the Severn, following the killing of a man in a riot, soldiers were quartered there and swivel guns were sited at the entrances of the town against the return of hungry 'colliers' and 'country people'.[5]

Raikes senior took care to make his readers fully aware of the seriousness of the situation and gave unreserved approval to the actions of the authorities. At the same time he seemed to be very conscious of the fears, suffering and dire distress of those driven to such lengths as rioting and he was prompt to give publicity to any efforts made to bring relief to the starving, in the hope that other wealthy people would be encouraged to do likewise. News of relief given in neighbouring counties like that from Leominster was inserted in his newspaper. 'Last week Thomas Johnes, of Croft Castle Esq., out of compassionate Regard to the present Wants and Distresses of his poor Neighbours, ordered Two fat Oxen to be killed, and divided amongst them, together with a proportionable Quantity of Corn; which was accordingly done, to the great Comfort and relief of necessitous Families.'[6]

Whether or not the well-to-do of Gloucester and district were influenced specifically by the newspaper reports it is not possible to determine, but they responded to the crisis and Raikes was able to announce: 'The Gentlemen of the City and Neighbourhood have begun a subscription for raising a Fund, to purchase, in distant Markets, a considerable Quantity of Corn, which, during the present high Prices of Grain, will be sold at a cheap Rate to the Poor of this City and such other Places as the Subscriber shall appoint: And it is not doubted that many Gentlemen, &c. will concur with them in their Design, by contributing, to the utmost of their Power towards the Promotion of so necessary and laudable an Undertaking.'[7]

Raikes senior gave front page coverage to letters and articles which revealed the desperate plight of the poor, 'half starved infants hanging on to their necessitous Parents with Cries for Food and Sustenance which pierce them to the heart'.[8] He printed in full a long article written by the 'Monitor Extraordinary'[9] entitled an 'Address to the legislative Power from the Poor Starving People of Britain, whose sufferings from the Present

High Price of Corn are paternally recommended to the Throne'. Unfortunately the author said nothing more constructive than that steps might be taken to stop 'the Abuse of Wheat in the Distillery,' and iterated the too-common observations of the time that 'Drunkenness is the Parent of Idleness' and 'Idleness is the Parent of Poverty'. Few practical ideas were contained in the other items sent to the printer, but among the most thoughtful of these was a letter from someone who signed himself 'Amicus'. His suggestions for 'Ways to lessen the present Want' included 'Obtaining the Lord's blessing on (their) Labours by breaking off (their) Sins' of 'Infidelity, Prophaneness, Corruption, Gaming and trifling away time', whilst at the same time strictly forbidding the export of corn, putting a total prohibition on the production of Malt Spirits, which, he argued, 'is wasting Corn to make Poison' and importing grain from abroad 'if any cheaper Markets could be found'. He also urged the 'Raising of any Sort of Eatables' and pointed out that 'Carrots sowed next Spring (would) be eatable Three Months before Harvest'. A final pertinent comment from Amicus (who could have been Raikes himself) was that 'at this Time of Want the Rich ought certainly to help their poor neighbours'. A letter of appreciation from Monmouth addressed to the printer and commencing, 'Sir, The Poor are much obliged to you for the Care you take in your Paper to represent their present Miseries' had the harrowing postscript, 'I have Reason to think some have already perished for want of Bread'.[10]

Throughout the winter and spring of 1757 people lived near starvation; rioting and pillaging occurred, and some of those responsible were arrested, tried, and capitally convicted, but then reprieved. Raikes was pleased to report on 19 February that for the poor of Gloucester City and environs, 'A considerable Sum of Money was received last week by Mr. Singleton in Guineas, Half Guineas, Crowns and Halfcrowns (many of which were sent to him) in order to relieve Hundreds of Poor Families in this City, and the Outer parts adjoining to it with Eleven penny Loaves of Bread at Seven pence Halfpenny Each – A charity calculated with Certainty to be laid out in Proper Food, and to cherish the Industrious Poor.'[11] Raikes also included the news from Bristol that two ships with 46,000 bushels of fine wheat had arrived at the port from Spain.[12]

The price of wheat reached its peak in late April, and, early in

May, Raikes assured his readers of an improvement in the situation, commended the magistrates upon their efforts to maintain order, and castigated those who were prepared to profit from the catastrophe. 'All our Accounts from adjacent Markets are full of the pleasing Prospects of the sinking Price of Grain . . . This, we flatter ourselves, will in a great measure prevent these Outrages and Insurrections which are become almost general amongst the turbulent, tho' greatly to be pitied, Poor. However, as the Suppressing of such illegal Proceedings is absolutely necessary to the Peace and Safety of the Community, we are confidently assured the Magistrates of this City are resolved to exert their Authority in protecting the Trade of the Market; which we hope will induce the Farmers to bring in their Grain . . . And, as we have undoubted Assurances that the great Stocks of Corn in the Country will in the End most certainly disappoint the avaricious Designs of those obdurate Wretches whose Hearts are Proof against the affecting Distresses of the Poor, the Farmers will find it as much to their own Interest as the publick Benefit to thresh out their Corn, and sell it at a moderate Price.'[13] It is impossible to say whether or not Raikes' exhortation was effective in persuading the farmers to bring their corn to market, but grain did begin to fall gradually in price.

Raikes senior roundly condemned the business dealings of a particularly worldly cleric in a full account of a disorder on 26 April, 1757. 'We . . . hear from Hereford,' wrote Raikes, 'that last Wednesday, the Poor of that Place assembled together in a very riotous Manner and seized a Waggon load of Wheat, which was intended to have been put on board a Vessel there, and sent to Bristol. The Wheat is said to have been the Property of a certain Clergyman in that County; and the Mob, being greatly exasperated on hearing that he had made a Practice of sending Grain in large Quantities to Bristol, to the very great Distress of the Poor of that Neighbourhood, cried out, No parson! No Badger![14] At last they tumbled the Grain out of the Waggon, opened the Sacks, and emptied them in the Market-place, from whence the old Women filled their Aprons, and carried it away . . . Tho' these Riots seem to be a growing Evil, and greatly to be discouraged by all Persons, yet in the present Instance very few seem concerned about the Doctor's Loss. And it is hoped that, for the future, this will put some Check to his trade of Badging, and teach him to be contented with acting in his proper Sphere, as a Clergyman, and not to defile that Holy Function.'[15]

Raikes, who took over the editorship of the *Gloucester Journal* on 12 July, 1757, seemed to have equally delighted to make public and commend the actions of the landowner whose tenant farmers had been more concerned with profit than humanity. 'We hear,' declared young Raikes, 'that a certain Gentleman near Ross, was so much offended at the iniquitous Proceedings and at the great Cruelty of the Farmers in that County, in refusing to sell Grain, in small Quantities to their own Workmen and to the industrious Poor, that he has given Notice to Two of his most considerable Tenants to quit their farms. [It is to be wished that all other Gentlemen in this County would imitate so worthy an Example, and likewise take into their serious Consideration the Calamities of the Poor in these hard times]'.[16]

Two other short passages in the *Gloucester Journal* during the elder Raikes' last year as editor and his son's final year of apprenticeship clearly reflect the father's outlook. One concerned pauper children. 'We hear Eight Poor Boys, lately sent from our (Gloucester City) Workhouse to the Marine Society at London, are all completely cloathed and fitted out by the said Society and entered with great cheerfulness, all together, on board the Furnace Sloop of War, at Woolwich – This is mentioned for the Honour of the Marine Society, and as an Encouragement to other Boys, who cannot be better provided for, to follow the Example.'[17] The second concerned those imprisoned for debt; 'The unfortunate Debtors confined in the County-gaol of Hereford do return their hearty and sincere Thanks to John Bridges Esq., of Tiberton in the said county, for his kind and generous distribution of Thirty Stone of Beef.'[18]

The edition of the *Gloucester Journal* dated Tuesday, 13 September, 1757, contains no reference to the passing of its founder and editor, but on at least one copy of the previous week's edition, written in ordinary handwriting are the sad words, 'This week died R. Raikes sen.' In his years as editor Raikes senior had constantly supported law and order and advocated and publicised good causes and opposed and condemned what was unjust and detrimental to the public interest. He had shown himself sympathetic to those in need. Fortunately for the poor and distressed, the newspaper continued under the eldest son in this long established tradition. In December, 1759, for instance, Raikes appealed successfully through the *Gloucester Journal* for money to help some 3,000 destitute French prisoners of war and over £33 was sent to Colonel Norborne Berkeley of the Gloucestershire Militia at Winchester.

Food shortages in the mid 1760's were even more serious than others already noted and early in September, 1766 Raikes cites an example of riotous weavers from the Stroud valleys marching to Gloucester to compel farmers to sell their wheat at 5s a bushel, the market price being 7s to 8s. The authorities took action and some of the weavers were arrested and committed to Gloucester gaol and the rest dispersed.[19] The measures taken by the county authorities were neither adequate nor sufficiently effective, and the industrious poor in the Stroud area were particularly hard hit, as Raikes showed: 'As the clothing part of the county cannot raise corn sufficient for its numerous inhabitants, it is in a degree dependent on remote parts for a weekly supply of many thousand bushels; but ever since the commotion, this supply has been withheld for fear of the mob; and now the poor wretches are almost perishing for want of sustenance; many of them have not tasted a morsel for several days.'[20]

The situation worsened, hungry mobs rioted in desperation, and some of their number were arrested. Raikes reported an increase in the number of prisoners in Gloucester gaol: 'Our gaol is filled with rioters that were brought in last week. Their number already amounts to thirty-five; many of whom are charged with atrocious breaches of the law.'[21] The disturbances were widespread and Raikes' reports indicate some of the terrible effects on poor families. In the Chepstow area men through fear of arrest abandoned their homes and were driven into vagrancy. 'The Dragoons quartered here (Chepstow)', said the *Gloucester Journal* correspondent, 'have had full employ this week past in bringing in more rioters. The number now in gaol is upwards of 60; but those who have fled their country upon this occasion, we are told exceed 400; many of whom have left wives and large families to be maintained by their parishes. – From the late rebellious spirit of the common people a melancholy train of evils is likely to ensue, both to themselves and their country.'[22]

Accounts of the horrors of human disaster such as famine, disorder, and public executions were irresistibly newsworthy in

Raikes' time and eighteenth century newspapers carried articles on these in abundance. It seems probable that during this period Raikes became involved in his first philanthropic labour – prison visiting. Raikes' knowledge of Gloucester prison in September, 1766 appears to have been gained from information received rather than personal experience, as we can see from his report of the precarious condition of some of the prisoners. 'There are now in our Castle fourteen or fifteen persons confined for small debts of £10 or £11. These poor men are in such distress that they are near perishing for want of sustenance: about a fortnight ago, one unfortunate man, they say, was actually starved to death there. Who in the full possession of the good things of this world, can refuse a small share to alleviate such a state of wretchedness?'[23] A week later Raikes was pleased to return the prisoners' thanks for the Charitable response to his appeal by the Right Hon., the Earl of Berkeley.

In December, 1766, Raikes reported that the number of prisoners in Gloucester Castle had greatly increased and included '96 rioters, 16 of whom were women and 29 other persons for various felonies'. On Saturday 13 December the Hon. Baron Perrot and Mr. Justice Aston arrived to try the prisoners. Dragoons were quartered in the city for the duration of the assize at which 'nine rioters received the sentence of death and seven were ordered to be transported'.[24] Raikes' editorial of 5 January, 1767 included the following passage based on information he had received. 'On Friday His Majesty's warrant came down for the execution of three of the rioters condemned at our special assizes, viz. Joseph Wildey, the fellow who untiled Mr. Chandler's house at Pakenhill (near Stroud), Stephen Cratchley for carrying a horn which he blew to collect the mob, and Anselm Prinn, one of the principals in demolishing the house near (Minchin) Hampton. The execution is fixed for Friday next, but the poor wretches, we are told, are so ill and weak, and so deeply affected with their sentence, that it is thought they will scarcely live to that day. Their behaviour is very decent and resigned.'[25]

On the day of the execution, Raikes probably visited the Castle and saw the prisoners for himself, judging from the detail and pathos in his description later. 'On Friday,' he wrote, 'three rioters, Cratchley, Wildey and Prinn, were executed pursuant to their sentence. Cratchley's behaviour before his death was uniformly steady, sensible and devout. He received the Sacrament at his own earnest request, and seemed to have attained the happy state of mind when death comes divested of his terrors. He said that he little thought his crime had been of so heinous a nature, and he hoped his countrymen would let the untimely fate of him and his companions have a due influence on their minds. Before he left the Castle he took affectionate leave of his wife and friends, and when at the gallows hastened the executioner to put an end to the business. Wildey seemed insensible; he was in a high fever, and had been in a delirium several days; and Prinn, who was a very ignorant lad, behaved with great decency and composure upon this solemn occasion.'[26]

Raikes was quick to warn those who might contemplate breaking the law. When, on the day following the executions, Saturday, 10 January, threatening letters were sent to landowners in Gloucester, Raikes pointed out in the next edition of his paper, only two days later, the dangers to the writers and any others who attempted to carry out the threats. The letter writers demanded that the landowners should compel their tenant farmers to sell their corn and other crops at moderate prices and those failing to do this would have their barns, corn stacks, even their houses, set on fire. The letters, Raikes said, produced a very different effect from that intended. They had raised the indignation of the recipients and made them feel that all they had done, and were doing, for the poor, and 'the great mercy' shown to rioters in general, was ill repaid. Raikes also pointed out possible repercussions upon prisoners in Gloucester gaol 'under sentence of death, and only respited during his Majesty's pleasure'. Having been informed of the matter, probably under interrogation by the authorities who were determined to identify the culprits, they had been thrown 'into the deepest affliction' in case 'at this critical juncture' the Royal mercy should be withdrawn 'just as it was extending towards them'. One of the landowners, and it might well have been Raikes himself because he owned land under tenancy, requested those responsible for the letters to consider the risks to themselves and to their friends who acted unlawfully, asked if they had fully explored legal means of obtaining redress of their grievances and begged them earnestly 'not (to) increase the misery to themselves and their country'.[27]

In the next edition of the *Gloucester Journal* Raikes became reassuring over relief for the poor, and even eloquent about the plans being devised in various parts of the country. 'It is most certain,' he wrote, 'that the spirit of charity, that now prevails in every part of the kingdom, former times had no idea of; – Schemes are meditating in this and all counties around us for supplying the industrious labourer and manufacturer with bread at a reasonable rate.'[28]

Even so Raikes must have been fully aware that farmers were insensitive to the cries of the poor and were prepared to sell their corn only when they decided the profits would be greatest and being reminded of this fact during the next week he upbraided them for their greed and heartlessness. On Monday, 26 January, he reported, 'Wheat rose considerably in our market on Saturday. The farmers say, jeeringly, that it is not their fault, 'tis the bakers and mealmen, who will give them the price; and they should be fools to refuse it, though a lower price would content them.' Raikes then made public one instance, 'a prelude (he feared) to many others where the charitable contributions have not been made', of 'the distress which (then reigned) in the country.' His specific purpose, he said, was so 'that the farmers, whilst they are drinking their toddy, and congratulating one another on the high price of corn, may not say they are ignorant of what the poor suffer'. Raikes hoped also that it would 'serve to quicken the attention of parish officers . . . that they may not be regardless of the duty of their office'. A surgeon and coroner of Stroud, one George Nayler, had addressed the following passage to the printer:

'Mr. Raikes, It having been represented to me by a clergyman of the neighbourhood of Moreton-Vallance, that a boy, about 12 years of age, was famished to death, I proceeded according to the rules of my office, and had the body taken up this day, and held an inquest on it; and the jury agreed, that the boy died for want of every necessary of life. – The boy's sister, who was a material evidence, declared upon oath, that her brother was starved, and that he had many times eaten coals and ashes from the hearth for want of food. Upon which I opened the body, and found the abdominal viscera perfectly sound; and upon opening the stomach, found a considerable quantity of coals and ashes, as described by his sister. His head was covered with lice, which in many places had penetrated even to his skull. His body was

extremely emaciated, that to me it was one of the most dismal
spectacles I ever beheld, scarcely skin to cover the bones. So that,
through the neglect of the parish officer, this poor boy must have
died of hunger; and many poor people, there is much reason to
believe, are dying of the same disease.'[29]

Action was taken by authorities and the better off to alleviate
the hunger of the poor, even if it was too late for those who had
already died. At a 'numerous meeting' in Gloucester of the
'Gentlemen, Clergy and Principal tradesmen . . . a subscription
opened for procuring bread and other provisions from home and
foreign markets . . . to sell to the poor on easy terms',[30] and figures later published by Raikes showed that during the winter
some 990 families were provided with 135,174lb of bread.[31] The
church also appears to have launched an appeal because Raikes
announced on 23 February, 1767, 'The Lord Bishop of the diocese
was lately most graciously pleased to receive £20 to alleviate the
distress of the poor of this city.'[32]

In the 'cloathing part of the county', the Stroud area, a voucher
system for relieving the poor had been devised in mid-January by
various subscribers. On application the poor were given vouchers
to take to a baker who had previously agreed to supply 12lb of
bread for 12d, the bakers then receiving from the relief fund a
further 4d for each 12lb supplied. Each poor family was allowed
to purchase 9lb of bread per head per week for adults, 6lb for
children.[33] Before the end of February some 10,000 poor people
had obtained bread by this arrangement.[34]

Petitions were sent to Parliament requesting that the export of
corn and its use by distillers should be prohibited and that free
import of corn should be permitted. The 'Steward, Bailiff and
Inhabitants of Cirencester' presented such a petition in December,
1766. The 'Aldermen, Sheriffs, Common Council and Principal
Inhabitants of the City of Gloucester' had despatched a petition
the previous January addressed specifically to Charles Barrow and
George Augustus Selwyn, the City's representatives in Parliament and, significantly, amongst the fifty-one signatures, those of
'Thomas Rich Stock'[35] and 'R. Raikes' appear together.

Hungry men continued to cause disturbances and at an assize
in Gloucester in March, 1767, five rioters 'were ordered to be
transported for life'.[36] Raikes was obviously pleased to state at the
end of the same month that, 'By authority from our Magistrates

we are assured, that a ship laden with foreign wheat is now bound for this port, and is daily expected in the river, by which it plainly appears that our account of the price of bread corn in this market has proved an encouragement to the importation of this commodity.'[37] Throughout the spring the columns of the *Glouces-ter Journal* contained arguments about the heartlessness of farmers and the honesty of mealmen and bakers and about the inconsistency in the sizes of measures used in retailing corn.

However, Raikes had a sense of humour which had been tick-led by a visitor to his printing office and he found space to describe the incident for his readers. 'A demure old Farmer,' said Raikes, 'came and observed on Saturday that he was afraid Bak-ers and Mealmen never read their Bible, but as he knew they always read the Newspaper, he desired a place might be given here to the following texts of scripture – Just balances, just weights, a just ephah, and a just hin, shall ye have: Levit. 19 v 36. Divers weights and divers measures, both of them are alike abomination to the Lord. Pro. XX 10.'[38]

Throughout the emergency, Raikes had staunchly supported the authorities, and, whilst having pity on the poor, appears not to have concerned himself with the cruelty of the sentences inflicted under the law. He was, in fact, proud when his news-paper became the means by which a lawbreaker was identified and apprehended. The *Gloucester Journal* of 15 June, 1767, printed Raikes' statement, 'On Wednesday se'night, in consequence of an advertisement in this Paper, the fellow for picking Mr. John Lench's pocket of 15 guineas, at the George, in Mitchel-Deane, in this county, was taken up at the King David, on St. Michael's Hill, Bristol, and committed to bridewell.' (A bridewell was an institution for petty offenders.)

The severity of the Penal Code was thought to act as a deterrent to crime. Some two hundred offences, ranging from petty theft to murder, were capital, and the executions took place in public, for the sickening horror of the spectacle was considered, as we have seen, a means of dissuading others from criminal acts and thereby risking the same punishment. Raikes' compassion lay in the pub-licity he gave to the appalling examples and in his role of prison visitor. The execution of two young mothers reveals the sheer barbarity of the law and the ignorance of those who administered it. It is understood today that a mother immediately after her con-

finement may not be held responsible for her actions and might
fatally injure her baby if proper care by others is not taken. This
could happen even where the finest medical care is available and
the mother has a loving husband and family. Consider now these
two cases reported by Raikes; probably both girls had suffered a
psychological trauma, if not physical brutality from all and sundry, during their pregnancy, 'On Monday last Elizabeth Grim-
mett was executed here for the murder of her bastard child. This
unhappy wretch was in great agonies at the approach of death,
and wept most bitterly as the cart drew away.'[39] The second poor
girl seems to have had few friends she could trust and to whom
she could turn for help. 'On Tuesday last ended the assizes at
Worcester, when Susannah Grigg, for the wilful murder of her
female bastard child, of which she delivered herself, about three
weeks ago, at Dudley, received sentence of death, and was
executed on Thursday.'[40]

Slightly more fortunate offenders, who escaped the gallows,
were transported to America, or the West Coast of Africa, or
Australasia, to serve their sentences. This usually meant enduring
a terrible journey, during which for the most part they were
chained in overcrowded holds, to serve their sentences, probably
for life, in a distant continent.[41] If they managed to escape and
return home and were recognised and arrested, they almost certainly would be hanged.

For lesser crimes those convicted were sometimes sentenced to
the hulks, a floating penitentiary on the Thames, from whence
they were employed in hard labour. At Gloucester Assizes in
March, 1778, a John Lloyd was sent to the hulks for three years
for stealing cloth, while in August the following year an Edward
Nail was given a five-year sentence for receiving stolen goods.
Those who considered sentence to a hulk more lenient than one
of transportation probably had no idea of the conditions on these
old vessels. John Howard, the prison reformer, did not publish
the horrors that he found on his first visit to the *Justitia*, one of
the hulks, in 1776, but he left a description in his answers to questions put to him by a Parliamentary Committee. J. B. Brown, his
chief biographer, quoted from the *Journals of the House of Commons*
as follows: 'Many (convicts) had no shirts, some no waistcoats,
some no stockings, and others no shoes. Several of them required
medical attendance but had none. By waiting to see their messes

weighed out, (Howard) ascertained that the broken biscuit actually given to them was green and mouldy, though that which the captain showed him as a sample was good and wholesome . . . In every other respect, the poor wretches were as miserably neglected. Even the sick who were only separated from the healthy, if any such there could be in this loathsome prison, by a few boards roughly nailed together, had nothing to sleep upon but bare decks. Their drink was water, and many of them told him in a whisper, lest their inhuman task-masters should overhear their complaints, that their meat was much tainted.'[42] Howard was pleased to see conditions improved on his next visit in 1778, although he said that they were still far from satisfactory.

Other forms of punishment meted out to convicts included branding, whipping, and placing in the pillory. Raikes reported that after the March Assize in Gloucester, 1778, 'Robert Williams, William Ricketts and William Young were for divers thefts . . . branded and ordered on board a man-of-war.'

Although Raikes was never critical about the harshness of sentences imposed he appears in the late sixties to have had a new awareness of, and greater concern for, those being punished under the law. He not only made known through his newspaper the plight of prisoners in Gloucester Castle, but he acted as agent to receive and distribute gifts of charity to them and then gradually became personally involved in attending to their welfare. In February, 1767 he published the contents of a letter which he had received signed 'A Friend', 'Sir, INCLOS'd is a £10 Bank-note which you are requested to apply to the relief of the prisoners in the castle of your city, in such a manner as you think may be most suitable to their respective wants, either in money, provisions, or cloathing, which is left to your discretion. As these poor people are shut up from the eyes and ears of those capable of relieving them, if their case was to be made more public, it might probably be the means of their receiving some further relief. Be pleased to acknowledge the receipt of this in your next Paper, and you will oblige.'

Along with this gift Raikes acknowledged the receipt of two guineas from, 'A Gentlewoman' and £4 1s 3d collected by a Mr Willis from his neighbours all donated 'for the same purpose', and replied, 'The Printer is happy in being the instrument of conveying relief to these distressed people. He has visited them several times, and enquired into their characters and wants, and has given orders for such necessary apparel as they stood most in need of. He has also set one man at liberty, who was kept in prison for fees that amounted only to 27s 6d; and shall in every respect endeavour to fulfil the intention of the donors, with all possible economy; of this they will be judges when he sets before them the particulars in which their money has been expended.'[43]

Tribute was paid to Raikes' efforts on behalf of the prisoners in Gloucester gaol by John Howard, in his famous work, *The State of the Prisons*. 'Of the felons, etc., in September and December, 1776, thirteen were transports: most of them were convicted at lent assize 1775. About twenty were fines; who, not having the county allowance, not any employment, were in September very pitiable objects indeed; half naked and almost famished. But in December their appearance was much altered. Mr. Raikes and other gentlemen took pity on them, and generously contributed towards the feeding and clothing them. Mr. Raikes continues his unremitting attention to prisoners.'

More than simply appealing for contributions to help feed, clothe, and sometimes release prisoners and seeing to it personally that gifts were used sensibly and to best effect, Raikes became an advocate of prison reform. The dreadful conditions in Gloucester Castle were described by Howard after his visit in 1773. 'The castle,' he stated, 'is also one of the county bridewells: yet only one court for all prisoners; and one day-room (eleven feet nine inches by ten feet seven), for men and women felons. The free ward for debtors is nineteen feet by eleven, which having no window, part of the plaster wall is broken down for light and air. The night room (the main) for men felons though up many stone steps, is close and dark; and the floor so ruinous, that it cannot be washed. Adjoining to the main, there are other night-rooms for fines, etc. These have also their separate day-room. The whole prison was much out of repair and had not been whitewashed for many years. The upper rooms were the bridewell; but at my last visit they were used for an infirmary. Many prisoners died here in 1773, and I generally saw some sick in this gaol . . . Only one sewer. No bath. Neither clauses against spiritous liquors, nor the Act for preserving the health of prisoners, are hung up.

'There is no separation of the women, or of the bridewell prisoners. The licentious intercourse of the sexes is shocking to decency and humanity. Many children have been born in this gaol.'[44]

Howard, a guest of Raikes, was admired by him, so it is not surprising that proposals for a new county bridewell were allotted space on the front page of the *Gloucester Journal*. An address (unsigned) 'To the worshipful JUSTICES of the PEACE and other Gentlemen of the county of Gloucester' printed in special small type filled more than a column in the edition of 9 March, 1778. The writer could well have been Raikes because he was fully acquainted with the conditions in Gloucester gaol, was sympathetic to Howard's views, and was skilful enough in approach, style, and choice of language to present a trenchant argument without giving offence to the reasonable. In the article emphasis was laid upon the 'extreme necessity' of those imprisoned for debt, because 'they (had) not a farthing allowed by the county for their sustenance'. It was further urged that whilst in the castle gaol, tools and materials could not be supplied 'lest they should furnish felons with them for means of escape or other mischief', but that, in a new bridewell, work could be provided to enable the prisoners to earn money for food. (Raikes himself observed that 'idleness was the parent of much mischief among them and that they quarrelled with one another because they had nothing else to do'.) Other points made were that the corruption of a first offender, 'a young creature, perhaps never taught a moral lesson, guilty of some petty theft' by the most incorrigible would be avoided and hence 'the perpetuation of villainy'. There is another pointer to Raikes as the probable writer of the article. It was stated that in many foreign prisons 'great care was taken' to give (the prisoners) moral and religious instruction, and reform their manners for their own and the public good. 'The Chaplain,' stated the writer 'not only performs public worship, but instructs the prisoners in private, and catechises them every week.' The infrequent attendance of the Revd James Evans, Chaplain of Gloucester prison, and the neglect of religious instruction for prisoners was observed by Howard during his visit. 'There is a small chapel, but all endeavours of the chaplain to promote the reformation among the prisoners must necessarily be defeated, by the inattention of the magistrates, and their neglect of framing and enforcing good regulations. Perhaps this is the reason the chaplain seldom attends.'[45] If discouragement from lack of con-

verts caused the chaplain to make but infrequent visits, Raikes
himself was prepared to take up the challenge. The Christian
beliefs expressed in the article would be those avowed by Raikes.
'And if the idea is delightful of having contributed to the relief of
a fellow creature afflicted with sickness and poverty, what ought
to be our satisfaction in reflecting that our bounty has rescued a
fellow Christian from perdition, eternal perdition; and that we
have rendered him an useful and happy member of society.'
Underneath the address Raikes, as editor, added in italics the
starred note, 'See Mr. Howard's excellent book on the state of
Prisons in England, Holland, &c. from which many of the above
remarks are taken.'

Tempering Raikes' humanity was a strict realism that law and
order were of paramount importance[46] and he accepted on the
part of authority, neither slackness nor sentimentality. The following week in his newspaper Raikes reported that 'Mr. Baron
Eyre, in his charge of the grand jury, informed them that a plan
(was) in contemplation for the punishment of criminals, by confining them to hard labour in workhouses to be erected for the
purpose. This (was) speedily to take place, and Gloucestershire,
Monmouthshire and Herefordshire (were) to form one district in
execution of this design.' And here the editor commented, 'We
hope the utility of the above schemes will be equal to the justice
of it, as nothing can be more fit, that crimes occasioned by idleness, extravagance and intemperance should be punished by confinement, abstinence and hard labour.'[47]

With great frequency Raikes continued his appeals for help for
the prisoners, particularly the debtors, as exampled on 3 August,
1778. 'The printer having expended the whole of the several sums
of money committed to his care for the relief of such of the prisoners in the county gaol, as are debarred from any allowance of
bread by the county, begs leave to recommend them to the
further compassionate regard of those who, together with the
inclination, have the ability to assist in mitigating the misery of
want and imprisonment.' Reiterating the fact that debtors relied
on private charity rather than county support Raikes appealed 'for
them, as they cannot appear to plead for themselves – Thirteen
are now in a deplorable state with the smallpox, two are dead,
and others it is supposed can scarcely recover – Benefactions for
their relief will be received by the printer.'[48]

As Raikes gradually became more closely involved with the prisoners, he began to engage in activities very akin to his later work in Sunday schools. He attempted that which the clergy had given up in despair, namely, to instruct and enlighten prisoners. He not only taught them himself, but he encouraged prisoners who were able to undertake the teaching of other prisoners; in fact, he appears to have organised a system which he was later to introduce into his Sunday schools. Above all he reflected upon the reasons why the prisoners had engaged in crime.

The principal evidence of Raikes' work in Gloucester prison is available to us today through the observations of his friend and first biographer, the Revd Samuel Glasse, which we quote in full, 'Whereas extreme ignorance was very properly considered by him as the principal cause of those enormities which brought (the prisoners) into their deplorable situation, precluding all hope of any lasting or real amendment from their punishment; his great desire was, if possible, to procure for them some moral and religious instruction. If among the prisoners, he found one that was able to read, he gladly made use of him to instruct his fellow-prisoners, encouraging his diligence and fidelity in this undertaking by pecuniary rewards, and procuring for him such other kinds of indulgence as his situation could admit of. Having thus put them in a method of improving their time, he has met with instances of persons, especially among the young offenders, who have attained to a competent proficiency in reading, which has served both as an amusement to them during their confinement, and as a recommendation of them in their restoration to the community.

'It may more easily be conceived than expressed, what that benevolent heart must have felt (and this pleasure he has often received) when he has heard the prisoner thank God, that by being detected in his crimes, apprehended, and imprisoned, he has had opportunities afforded him of learning that good, which otherwise he would probably have never known in his whole life. The choice of books being judiciously made, and religious instruction going hand-in-hand with other information, the teacher himself has often learnt while he was instructing others, and, from the very nature of his employment, became imperceptibly a better man.

'But the care of this philanthropist was not confined merely to the business of literary improvement; it was not less his desire to form their hearts, if it were possible, to sentiments of kindness to each other. Indeed, it was one of his principal endeavours to subdue in them, if it were possible, that savage ferocity of temper and behaviour which only served to render their situation more hateful and intolerable. Observing that idleness was the parent of much mischief among them, and that they quarrelled with one another because they had nothing else to do, he endeavoured to procure employment for such as were willing, or even permitted, to work.'[49]

Evidence from another contemporary source indicates a link between Raikes' philanthropic labours in Gloucester prison and his work in Sunday schools, although Raikes himself maintained that the founding of Sunday schools in Gloucester was accidental. John Howard, after he had paid one of his visits to Gloucester in 1782, included this footnote in the third edition of his *State of Prisons*, published in 1784. 'This gentleman (Raikes) is also the founder of a benevolent and useful institution (Sunday schools) for the children of this city . . . which, by his attention and liberal encouragement, have had happy effect in improving the morals of the younger classes; many of whom now look up to their kind benefactor with great esteem and affection. Perhaps Mr. Raikes's frequent visits to the castle suggested to him this plan, as the last means of preventing youth from coming there.'

There is further evidence that Raikes, through his work in Gloucester prison being brought, as he was, face to face with the distress of the criminal prisoners, saw the need of social training and discipline. The daughters of William King, a woollen card merchant of Dursley, a village fifteen miles south of Gloucester, both contended that it was their father who had convinced Raikes of the need to establish a Sunday school for children who ran wild in the streets of Gloucester. King, who liked children and was noted for his goodwill and generosity, had established a Sunday school in his own factory in 1774, later to be transferred to the Tabernacle, Dursley, where he was a church leader. One of his principal reasons for gathering the children together and giving them religious training and teaching them to read, appears to have been to protect them from the temptations which could lead to imprisonment and execution. King, a man of great compassion, a convert of George Whitefield and admirer of John Howard, frequently visited Gloucester gaol to bring such comfort as he was able to those condemned to death. It appears that King, on business in Painswick, learned that two prisoners in Gloucester Castle were to suffer the death penalty. He went at once to Gloucester, intending to spend the night with the condemned men, but was refused admittance by the jailer who considered this inadvisable as the men were 'desperate characters'. King stayed the night in Gloucester and called on his friend Raikes, the two having become acquainted during their visits to the Castle. As they 'walked together towards the Island (an area between two branches of the River Severn and adjacent to the County gaol) and seeing lads at different sports', King observed that it was a pity the Sabbath should be so desecrated. Raikes was then said to have asked, 'Mr. King, how is it to be altered?' to which question King is alleged to have answered, 'Sir, if Sabbath schools were begun so as to give the poor education it would be the means of great good. I have endeavoured to open one myself with the help of a faithful journeyman of mine, but from multitude of business through the week I could not attend as I wished.' Raikes is said to have replied, 'Mr. King, it will not do for the Dissenters to do it; it must be by the Church.'[50] This remark was not perhaps the snub it would appear to be when looked at in the context of the times. Raikes would no doubt be sympathetic to the teaching of his bishop, William Warburton, who disliked the activities of dissenters, but this did not prevent his friendship with a Calvinist Methodist. Raikes himself makes no mention of the conversation and there is some confusion about the date at which it was supposed to have taken place.

The conclusion seems certain, however, that Raikes, whilst engaged in his charitable labours with prisoners, gave serious reflection to the reasons for their having to be brought to such melancholy consequences. Without doubt he saw that in many cases their misdemeanours were the result of ignorance alone, and that if instruction and enlightenment were not provided, many more poor people would be in the same pitiful state. When calling for the establishment and support of Sunday schools Raikes argued forcibly that 'the lower class of people, in a few years, would exhibit a material change of character and justify the superior policy which tends to prevent crimes rather than punish them.'[51] From his philanthropic work in Gloucester prison was to stem, not his motivation for founding Sunday schools, but his championship of them.

NOTES

[1] G. A. Cranfield, *The Development of a Provincial Newspaper 1700–1760* (1962) p 48
[2] *Gloucester Journal* 25 January, 1725
[3] Ibid 4 July, 1757
[4] See page 23
[5] *Gloucester Journal* 14 December, 1756; 28 December, 1756
[6] Ibid
[7] Ibid 25 January, 1757
[8] Ibid 15 February, 1757; 25 January, 1757; 1 February, 1757; 8 February, 1757
[9] An authority so far unidentified
[10] *Gloucester Journal* 15 February, 1757
[11] Ibid 22 February, 1757
[12] Ibid 8 March, 1757
[13] Ibid 10 May, 1757
[14] Badger: a corn dealer, a middleman buying from farmers and reselling.
[15] *Gloucester Journal* 3 May, 1757
[16] Ibid 6 August, 1757
[17] Ibid 15 February, 1757
[18] Ibid 26 April, 1757
[19] Ibid 15 September, 1766
[20] Ibid 6 October, 1766
[21] Ibid 20 October, 1766
[22] Ibid 27 October, 1766
[23] Ibid 8 September, 1766
[24] Ibid 22 December, 1766
[25] Ibid 5 January, 1767
[26] Ibid 12 January, 1767
[27] Ibid
[28] Ibid 19 January, 1767
[29] Ibid 26 January, 1767
[30] Ibid
[31] Ibid 27 April, 1767
[32] Ibid 23 February, 1767
[33] Ibid 19 January, 1767
[34] Ibid 23 February, 1767
[35] Thomas Rich Stock, father of the Revd Thomas Stock.
[36] *Gloucester Journal* 30 March, 1767
[37] Ibid
[38] Ibid 23 March, 1767
[39] Ibid 23 March, 1778
[40] Ibid 13 March, 1780
[41] Those having served their sentences had little hope of finding the means by which to return.
[42] J. B. Brown, *Memoirs of the Public and Private Life of John Howard the Philanthropist* p 232, quoted by E. C. S. Gibson, *John Howard* (1901) pp 106, 107
[43] *Gloucester Journal* 23 February, 1767

[44] J. Howard, *The State of the Prisons* pp 216, 217

[45] Ibid p 217

[46] A view common to most men of property and influence in the eighteenth century.

[47] *Gloucester Journal* 16 March, 1778

[48] Ibid 23 November, 1778

[49] Samuel Glasse, *Gentleman's Magazine* 1788 Vol LVIII pp 12, 13

[50] M. Oldland (daughter of William King), *Letter* 5 March, 1863 quoted in J. H. Harris, *Robert Raikes: The Man and his Work* p 150, also in H. Y. J. Taylor, *Robert Raikes and the Sunday Schools; A Collection of Newspaper Articles and Letters* (Vol 14315)

[51] Raikes, *Letter* 7 October, 1786

Chapter 4

FOUNDER OF SUNDAY SCHOOLS

Robert Raikes' own account of the setting up of his Sunday schools, written in a letter only three years after their foundation, made it clear that their establishment was accidental. When Samuel Colbourne, the then Mayor of Gloucester, received a letter from a Richard Townley of Belfield, a Squire and Magistrate of Rochdale[1] asking for information about Sunday schools (perhaps with a view to founding similar institutions in Rochdale), he passed it on to Raikes who replied as follows:

'Gloucester, November 25th 1783

Sir,

My friend, the Mayor, has just communicated to me the letter which you have honoured him with, enquiring into the nature of the Sunday schools. The beginning of this scheme was entirely owing to accident. Some business leading me one morning into the suburbs of the city, where the lowest of the people (who are principally employed in the pin-manufactory) chiefly reside, I was struck with concern at seeing a groupe of children, wretchedly ragged, at play in the street. I asked an inhabitant whether those children belonged to that part of the town, and lamented their misery and idleness. – "Ah! Sir, said the woman to whom I was speaking, could you take a view of this part of the town on a Sunday, you would be shocked indeed; for then the street is filled with multitudes of these wretches, who, released on that day from employment, spend their time in noise and riot, playing at chuck and cursing and swearing in a manner so horrid, as to convey to any serious mind an idea of hell, rather than any other place. We have a worthy clergyman; said she, curate of our parish, who has put some of them to school; but upon the sabbath, they are all given up to follow their inclinations without restraint, as their parents, totally abandoned themselves, have no idea of instilling into the minds of their children principles, to which they themselves are entire strangers."

This conversation suggested to me, that it would be at least a harmless attempt, if it were productive of no good, should some little plan be formed to check this deplorable profanation of the sabbath.'

The suburb of Gloucester in which Raikes had his business that morning was a lower class district known as St Catherine's Meadows, near the River Severn. Raikes was said to be seeking to employ the services of a gardener, who was not at home when he called, and the person to whom he was talking was the gardener's wife.[2]

Three points of major significance emerged from the conversation which seemed to have influenced Raikes in the course of action he took: the size of the problem, the specific day when the nuisance reached its peak, and the solution which the 'worthy clergyman' had found for the problem by putting 'some of them to school'.

The chief point of concern was the 'multitudes of wretches'. It is a fact of life that in every generation the adults find fault with the behaviour of the young, but Raikes knew the woman was neither exaggerating nor showing excessive prejudice, having seen plenty of examples himself and realising the dangers of neglect amongst the children of the poor.

It has been alleged, for instance, that Raikes became very much annoyed when rowdy children played hopscotch, five-stones and chuck, outside the window of his office in Bolt Lane on Sundays, when he wanted peace and quiet to read the proofs of the next issue of his paper. As he put it later, however, it was the 'crowds of children . . . engaged in noise and riot . . . to the extreme annoyance of all decent people'[3] of which Raikes had become increasingly aware.

The second point of importance was that the disturbance reached its height on Sundays. Concentration of workers in factories created new social problems, and working conditions took little account of the physical and physiological needs of adults, much less those of children. After six long, wearisome days in performing monotonous, routine operations in the pin factory, such pent up reserves of energy as were left in the young worker would inevitably be released in vociferous play. When the factory closed on Sunday the opportunity for this occurred and the language of the children, swearing and the use of profane oaths, had been learned from their elders.

Factory life was detrimental to family relationships. The parents themselves were described as 'abandoned'. In contrast with the domestic industries where the children worked with, and under, the supervision of their parents, and where the children's responsibilities and activities could be varied from work on the particular craft to collecting kindling and attending to the pigs or cow on the common pasture, so giving opportunity for them to romp and play, factory employment was confining, dulling, restrictive, coarsening, even brutalising. Parents were as much at the mercy of factory overseers as were their children, and not infrequently powerless to appeal against unjust, even cruel, disciplinary measures taken against them. Both parental influence and filial regard were weakened. Depravity left no ground for the growth of respect and pride within the family. Raikes was fully aware that obscenity and profanity are not inborn but he believed that indulgence in these often led to other kinds of social irresponsibility and infringements of the law, the consequences of which have been shown. However onerous his personal commitments, Raikes, having acknowledged the problem, determined to attempt a remedy.

The woman's third observation that the Revd Thomas Stock had founded schools for some of the children obviously stirred Raikes' imagination. He was well able to afford to pay the teachers himself and could count on help and advice from others with experience of such an enterprise. The burden of such a commitment would lie in the demands made on his time. He still had his business to run, his newspaper to edit, and he was a family man, with a son and seven daughters ranging from Caroline, aged one year, to Robert Powell, aged eleven. Even if Anne, his wife, did not expect his unstinting attention for herself and the children, domestic affairs would be bound to make demands on him.

Having made the decision to establish Sunday schools Raikes acted promptly. His letter to Richard Townley continued: 'I then enquired of the woman, if there were any decent, well-disposed women in the neighbourhood, who kept schools for teaching to read. I was presently directed to four: to these I applied, and made an agreement with them, to receive as many children as I should send on the Sunday, whom they were to instruct in reading and in church catechism. – For this I engaged to pay them each a shilling for their day's employment. The women seemed pleased with this proposal. I then waited on the clergyman before mentioned and imparted to him my plan; he was so much satisfied with the idea, that he engaged to lend his assistance, by going round to the schools on a Sunday afternoon, to examine the progress that was made, and to enforce order and decorum among such a set of little heathens.'

Raikes was fortunate in that numerous precedents had been set, and wide experience gained in schooling the children of the poor, which would have helped strengthen his resolve. Weekday schools and Sunday schools had been established and many were in existence when Raikes and Stock founded their Sunday school in Gloucester.

The effectiveness of the school as a civilising agency had been greatly in evidence in Gloucestershire earlier in the eighteenth century. Many charity schools had been established throughout the kingdom, a number in connection with the Society for Promoting Christian Knowledge (SPCK). One of the five founder members of the Society, who had attended the inaugural meeting in London on 8 March, 1698, was Colonel Maynard Colchester, a Gloucestershire squire. The Colonel was a pioneer of popular education. Colchester's charity schools were founded at Mitcheldean and Oxenhall and in the Westbury hamlets of Elton, Gatwick, Northwood and Rodley. He also subscribed to schools at Coleford, Newent and Newland. He was given the special task by the original members of the SPCK of considering 'how to further and promote that good design of erecting catechetical schools'.[4] Edward Fowler, Bishop of Gloucester, joined the SPCK in June, 1699, being the first bishop to do so, and gave his support to those of his clergy who founded schools. In November of the same year the SPCK circulated a letter to selected clergymen in England and Wales urging them to follow the lead given in the metropolis, by inviting contributions for the establishment of schools for the children of the poor from benevolent people in their respective parishes. A 'score of men, mainly parish clergy'[5] responded to the appeal and joined with Colonel Colchester in pioneering elementary education in the city of Gloucester and in other towns and villages of the county, Cheltenham, Prestbury, Dursley and Cam, Newent, Newland, Tewkesbury and Wotton-under-Edge.

Although the objectives of the SPCK were multifarious, the aims for its charity schools were religious, moral and social, and the organisation, regulation and supervision of the schools were the responsibility of the governors – trustees and local subscribers. Some of these philanthropists displayed missionary zeal in gathering into their schools the most beggarly, destitute, ill-mannered, even 'vicious', children from the most wretched and 'evil'[6] homes and attempted to instil into them clean habits, a sense of decency, respect for their betters and some acquaintance with the scriptures. The 1707 and 1711 issues of the annual, official SPCK *Account of Charity Schools lately erected in England, Wales and Ireland* set out explicitly what it was hoped would be achieved in these schools.

The 'chief design' was 'the knowledge and practice of the Christian religion as professed and taught in the Church of England'. The Master's 'chief business' was 'to instruct the children . . . in the Church Catechism'. He was first required to 'teach them to pronounce distinctly and plainly' and then 'explain it to the meanest capacity by the help of The Whole Duty of Man'. This was to be 'done constantly twice a week, (so) that everything in the Catechism may be the more perfectly repeated and understood'. The Master was also expected to 'take particular care of the manners and behaviour of the poor children . . . to teach them true spellings of words and distinction of syllables, with points and stops, which is necessary to true and good reading'. Instruction in writing and such arithmetic as would 'fit them for service or apprentices' was provided for boys, whilst girls were taught to 'knit their stockings and gloves, to mark, sew, make and mend their cloaths, and several learn to write and some to spin their cloaths'.[7]

In Colonel Colchester's largest school, near his residence and water gardens in Westbury-on-Severn, eighty children were in attendance in 1697, most of whom were pleased to accept gifts of bread and some were provided with clothing. The school was equipped with Testaments, copies of the Whole Duty of Man, hornbooks, primers, and writing books: details of these resources, the names and ages of the children and the names of their teachers and the payments they received were recorded and can still be read in the Public Records Office.

Although by the accession of George III (1760) the early

enthusiasm had flagged and the charity schools declined in efficiency and numbers, some disappearing after the death of their
founders, the SPCK continued its work and the experience
gained in organising schools for the teaching of poor children was
not lost and, perhaps more importantly, textbooks, manuals of
exercises and literature for children continued to be published.
Similarities in the functioning of the charity schools and the Sunday schools were very evident and this was hardly surprising
since both institutions were established with similar aims: to
ameliorate virtually the same problems. Charity school and Sunday school supporters were very much akin, being religious
people of conscience. Sometimes the Sunday school teacher also
taught in a weekday school.

Even if hesitant in making optimistic statements about the outcome of his venture Raikes might have nursed visions of the
Sunday school children becoming like the charity school children
portrayed in William Blake's *Songs of Innocence* written in 1789.
The practice had been instituted in 1782 that on the Thursday of
each Whitweek the children from London and Westminster charity schools should attend services in St Paul's Cathedral.

'Twas on a Holy Thursday, their innocent faces clean,
The children walking two and two, in red and blue and
    green . . .
O what a multitude they seem'd, these flowers of London
    town!
Seated in companies they sit with radiance all their own.
The hum of multitudes was there, but multitudes of lambs,
Thousands of little boys and girls raising their innocent hands.
                                                    Holy Thursday

However the fact that Raikes was an older and more practical
man, with an experience of life very different from that of Blake,
would sober his outlook, since he seems to have had some mis-
givings about any success he might achieve in filling the schools
or of effecting any change in the children's behaviour.

Raikes could in fact take encouragement from the work under-
taken in those Sunday schools which had been established in earlier times. He had ready access to information about the
approaches used by those who had tackled the same problem
both in charity and in Sunday schools. The idea of instructing

children in the Christian religion on Sundays was not exclusive to any particular denomination, nationality, or period, and the devoted service of those who founded Sunday schools before Raikes is worthy of consideration and recognition. From a wealth of examples the following may be singled out by their concern for religious teaching.

The Revd Joseph Alleine, a nonconformist, puritan clergyman, was a spirited teacher of the young. Born in 1633 in Devizes, Wiltshire, he studied at Corpus Christi College, Cambridge, and became curate of St Mary Magdalene's Church, Taunton, in 1655. Seven years later he was one of two thousand beneficed clergymen who resigned their livings rather than seek the episcopal ordination required to avoid being deprived of their livings under the Act of Uniformity. For continuing his ministry he suffered imprisonment for flouting laws designed to deter expelled ministers from forming their own congregations. As a result of his imprisonment and consequent illness, Alleine was so physically disabled that he had to be carried or to hobble about on crutches. In spite of this, in Bath, whence he had been borne in a litter, he gathered some sixty or seventy children together on Sundays and gave them religious instruction. He died in 1668, aged 35.

Robert Frampton, of whom, as a younger preacher, Samuel Pepys once commented, 'The truth is he preaches the most like an apostle that ever I heard man, and it was much the best time I ever spent in my life at church',[8] catechised and instructed children on Sundays. Frampton, the non-juring Bishop of Gloucester, although deprived of his bishopric in 1689 following his refusal to take the oath of allegiance to William III, still attended the parish church on Sunday mornings and in the afternoons carefully explained the curate's morning sermon to the children to facilitate their understanding.

Sunday schools were also started in America in the eighteenth century. John and Charles Wesley and two of their friends sailed for America in 1735, where John became minister in the parish of Savannah. Sensible of the children's need of education he set up a day school of which one of his travelling companions, Mr Delamotte, the son of a London merchant, took charge. Delamotte, a well-educated young man, besides teaching secular subjects also gave religious instruction to his pupils, and on Sundays, before the evening services, John Wesley made it one of his regular duties to meet children and reinforce this teaching by further elucidating Bible texts, and hearing them recite the Catechism. Also in the New World, a few years later, in the settlement of Ephrata, Lancaster, Pennsylvania, one Ludwig Hacker founded a Sunday school for the children of the German Seventh-Day Baptists. This school continued to function until September, 1777, when the schoolroom was commandeered as a hospital after the Battle of Brandywine.

Many Sunday schools had been established in the British Isles in the eighteenth century, some long before and others about the time Raikes and Stock embarked upon similar enterprises. A brief sketch, in chronological order, reveals how widely situated the Sunday schools were and the very devoted service of some of their founders. One David Lambert conducted a Sunday school in Berkshire in 1710 and a contemporary of Colonel Colchester, Mrs Catherine Boevey (1669–1726),[9] the beautiful, wealthy owner of Flaxley Abbey in the Forest of Dean, Gloucestershire, taught and catechised the children of her charity school on Sundays. Amongst the rewards Mrs Boevey gave to the poor children was 'sixpence' at Christmas and a 'beef and pudding' dinner on Sundays. The children took turns to dine at the Abbey, six of them having this privilege each week.

The first Sabbath evening school in Scotland is recorded as being opened in 1760 by a Mr Blair, the Presbyterian Minister of Brechin, perhaps influenced by the teachings of John Knox (c1514–72) the Scottish religious reformer, who encouraged special religious instruction for the young.

An account exists of the Sunday school opened by the Revd Theophilus Lindsey in Catterick, Yorkshire, about 1764. 'At two o'clock, before the commencement of the afternoon service, Mr. Lindsey devoted an hour in the church every Sunday, alternately, to catechising the children of the parish and to expounding the Bible to the boys of a large school which was at the time kept in the village. The number of boys generally amounted to about one hundred, who formed a circle round him: himself holding a Bible open in his hand, with which he walked slowly round, giving it regularly in succession to the boys, each reading in his turn, the passage about to be explained. This method, accompanied by frequently recapitulating what had been said, and by asking the boys questions relating to it, kept them very attentive; and the good effects of these labours proved, in many cases, apparent in after life.'[10] Also on Sunday evening, after the service, Mr Lindsey instructed 'different classes of young men and women' in his study. At the same time in another room in their house his wife taught 'two classes of children, boys and girls alternately'.[11] (Later in life, when he moved to London, there were many occasions when he ran into former Sunday school scholars who expressed their gratitude to him for the teaching they had received.)

Inspired by Lindsey's example a Mrs Cappe, née Harrison, started a Sunday school at Bedale in 1765. Her own narrative provides us with an insight into the difficulties confronting those engaged in such an enterprise. 'I established a sort of Sunday school there collecting a number of poor children, whom I assisted in learning to read, giving them books, etc., teaching them Dr. Watts's shorter catechism, together with the devotional hymns, and endeavouring to give them such general instruction as might enable them to read their Bible with more intelligence. I had no place in which to receive them but the back kitchen, which being so small, we were inconveniently crowded; but they grew attached to me and I liked to attend; and in order to prevent confusion, I divided them into three classes, who succeeded each other: so that on the Sunday I was occupied by a succession of children nearly the whole day, except the time which was spent at church.'[12] And in her single-handed labours neither encouragement nor help was forthcoming. Of this Mrs Cappe wrote, 'I could not prevail upon any of the young people in the town, the daughters of the tradesmen or others, to contribute in any way towards my Sunday School.'[13]

A young lady Methodist, Miss Hannah Ball, of High Wycombe, Buckinghamshire, who started a Sunday school there in 1769 and took the children to services in the parish church, experienced the challenge of working with neglected, unruly youngsters. John Wesley visiting the school in October that year referred to her charges as 'a lively congregation'. From her letter to Wesley in 1770 we can appreciate the strength of the religious motives of the twenty-two year old Miss Ball: 'The children meet twice a week – every Sunday and Monday. They are a wild little company, but seem willing to be instructed. I labour among them, earnestly desiring to promote the interest of the Church of Christ.'[14] This resolute lady continued to run the school for many years.

In 1770 the Revd Dr Thomas Kennedy, Curate of Bright Parish Episcopal Church in County Down, Ireland, being concerned over the smallness of his congregation arranged, with the help of a member of his church and the parish clerk, to assemble a mixed group of young people for singing sessions on Sundays. Gradually the reading of psalms and scripture lessons was introduced and as this proved acceptable the boys and girls were persuaded to bring, if possible, Bibles from home, and then instruction was given in what was read. Taking full advantage of the success achieved, Kennedy invited children of other denominations to join the group and soon Episcopalians, Methodists, Presbyterians and Roman Catholics were sitting together in the singing class. Over the next eight years this assembly developed into a Sunday school.

Another Sunday school of much humbler origin was formed at Little Lever near Bolton in 1775 as the result of the efforts of James Hey, locally known as 'Old Jemmy o' th' Hey', who was employed winding bobbins for weavers. Initially he taught the 'poor "bobbin" or "draw" boys' to read and spell, but later older boys and girls came to be instructed. As there appears to have been 'no place of worship in the locality'[15] and the number of his pupils was growing rapidly he agreed to teach them on Sundays and thanks to the generosity of Adam Crompton, a paper manufacturer, and others of his acquaintance whom he persuaded to contribute, funds and books were provided for the school. A large room in a neighbour's house was lent to James Hey for the purpose and in place of a bell he used an old brass pestle and mortar with which to call in the young people waiting in the lane outside.

Reference can be found to other Sunday schools which were in existence at the time Raikes decided to establish his in Gloucester. As he was fond of reading religious works he might have read *A Plea for Religion*, a popular work written by the Revd David Simpson, Minister of Christ Church, Macclesfield. He might also have learned of Mr Simpson's Sunday school, commenced in 1778, in which, under his direction, paid teachers were employed. On certain evenings in the week the children were taught in private houses and on Sundays given further instruction and taken to church. This school flourished and in 1786 four hundred and twelve children were in attendance and the expenditure that year

was £123 18s 0d.[16] Raikes certainly corresponded with the Revd
John Marks Moffatt, Minister of Forest Green Chapel, Nailsworth, Gloucestershire, 'a quiet, studious, unobtrusive man' who
had been teaching the children of his congregation on Sundays
for some six years before Raikes formed his 'little plan to check
the profanation of the Sabbath'.

These incipient developments in the provision of schools for
the children of the poor, which accorded with the spirit of the
age, all took place before Raikes and his co-worker, the Revd
Thomas Stock, planned their first Sunday school in 1780. For
some reason Raikes recorded the subsequent events incorrectly
and also omitted to mention 'the Clergyman's' financial contribution. It seems inconceivable that a businessman, as shrewd and
methodical as Raikes, would make such arrangements without
first consulting others better informed than himself on the
abilities of private adventure schoolteachers or dames.

The Revd Thomas Stock's own account published in a letter on
2 February, 1788, differed slightly from that of Raikes: 'The undertaking originated in the parish of St. John's, in this city, of which
I was curate. The fact is as follows: Mr. Raikes meeting me one
day by accident at my door, and, in the course of the conversation, lamenting the deplorable state of the lower classes of mankind, took particular notice of the situation of the poorer children.
I had made, I replied, the same observation, and told him if he
would accompany me into my own parish we would attempt to
remedy the evil. We immediately proceeded to the business, and,
procuring the names of about ninety children, placed them under
the care of four persons for a stated number of hours on the Sunday. As minister of the parish, I took upon me the principal
superintendence of the schools and one third of the expense.' The
meeting obviously was not accidental from Raikes' point of view:
he had a definite purpose when they met.

Raikes was very fortunate in having a man of the calibre of the
Revd Thomas Stock willing to join him in the enterprise. Stock, a
native of Gloucester, had a more intimate knowledge of the parish and the needs of his parishioners than Raikes. He had a considerable degree of sympathy for the poor which was reflected in
their regard for him. Moreover his insistence on making a financial contribution amounting to a weekly two shillings was a far
greater sacrifice than double that amount would have been for

Raikes. At thirty Stock had scholarship, teaching experience, and a knowledge of children, teachers, and school organisation which must have proved invaluable. His university education at Oxford began at seventeen and after taking an M A he became a fellow of Pembroke College. He obtained preferment to the curacy of the village of Ashbury in Berkshire where in 1777 he established a Sunday school, giving religious instruction to the children of the parish. The year following he came to Gloucester, having been appointed Headmaster of the Cathedral School. He also became Curate of St John's and Hempstead Churches, and Vicar of Glasbury, Breconshire, the Bishop of St David's being 'pleased to disperse with (his) residence (in Glasbury) in order to enable him to continue the care of his school'.[17] For the children of the parishes of Leigh and Hempstead, Stock is said to have established a reading school. In 1787, after obtaining preferment 'to the rectory of St. John the Baptist, (and) to the perpetual curacy St. Aldate',[18] he resigned his post at the Cathedral School.

Raikes and Stock worked together in the selection and employment of the teachers. No special qualifications were required and four people were found who were presumably able and willing to catechise the children, teach them to read, and take them to church. It seems likely that each teacher had some experience of teaching in a dame-school or private adventure school and being members of the 'lower orders' themselves, would appreciate the arduousness of their task, because it was the intention of the two Sunday school founders to send them children from the poorest homes, the ragged, hard-swearing, ignorant and ill-disciplined.

The provision of any purpose-built accommodation would have been out of the question and a room, usually a parlour, of the house of the teacher or a neighbour, sufficed. One of the first schools appears to have been established at the home of Mrs James King in St Catherine's Street, in July, 1780,[19] after Mr Stock had received her agreement to accept the post of teacher and the payment of 1s 6d for each Sunday. Unfortunately, Mrs King died three years later, but her husband showed great spirit in undertaking his wife's responsibilities as the teacher. Of the exact location of the other three Sunday schools opened by Raikes and Stock there exists no definite evidence. A Mrs Brabant kept a Sunday school in Oxbody Lane; a Mr and Mrs Bretherton were employed to keep another Sunday school in Hare Lane; a Mrs

Roberts was the mistress of a Sunday school held in the back premises of 103 Northgate Street, a Mr Tanner is said to have been the master of a Sunday school in St John's Parish and a Mrs Lea the mistress of one in St Aldate's. It is also recorded that a Sunday school was opened in St Aldate's Square in the house of the sexton of the church, a Mr Trickey, and one in a house in Leather Bottle Lane, notorious as one of the worst areas in the city, but whether Mrs Lea or Mr Tanner were the teacher of the last two mentioned has not been ascertained.

Raikes' first Sunday school, of which he made no particular mention, was opened in Sooty Alley, Littleworth, opposite the city prison: a slum area in which chimney-sweeps lived. Charles Cox, a native of Gloucester, aged nearly eighty-seven when interviewed in 1862, remembered that at the age of five he had attended this school with another twelve or fourteen boys under the charge of 'a woman named Meredith'.[20] It would appear from the available evidence that for some reason this school was closed ('Mrs. Meredith was apparently not strong enough on the nerves for those wild untrained Arabs of the city' contended J. H. Harris), and most of the boys were transferred to a school run by a Mrs Mary Critchley. Mrs Critchley, previously a regular school-mistress and known for her ability to cope with rough boys, had been prevailed upon by Raikes to open a Sunday school. This she did when subsequently she moved from Littleworth to a house on the corner of Southgate Street and Grey Friars opposite St Mary de Crypt Church. Initially her school was a mixed one, but later she taught only girls and her husband became master of the boys' Sunday school which was held in the house next door. Charles Cox is recorded as having stated that while living in Mr Stock's parish he was transferred to a school newly opened by Stock in Dolphin Lane and with a Mr Bamford as teacher.[21]

Visiting the homes of the parents and prevailing upon them to send their children to the Sunday school was a task likely to prove more difficult for a layman than a man of the cloth, although even for a clergyman such visits were not always without risk of unpleasantness, but Raikes took his full share of visiting. One couple, two of whose children aged ten and eleven years respectively had been committed to Gloucester prison for robbing the till of a local grocer, had previously been invited to send their children to Sunday school, and had replied that 'they

could teach them better things at home'.[22] Raikes was fully aware
of such reaction as is demonstrated in the following report: 'When
the Minister of the parish, like the good shepherd that cometh for
his sheep, kindly warned the father of keeping his children in a
state of ignorance, and irreligion, his pastoral care was requited
with insolence and abuse.'[23]

However, one senses that Raikes was not averse to confronting
poor families in their own homes. 'With regard to the parents,' he
wrote in 1785, 'I went round to remonstrate with them on the
melancholy consequences that must ensue from so fatal a neglect
of their children's morals. They alleged that their poverty
rendered them incapable of cleaning and clothing their children
fit to appear either at school or at church. But this objection was
obviated by a remark that if they were clad in a garb fit to appear
in the streets I should not think it improper for a school calculated
to admit the poorest and most neglected. All that I required were
clean faces, clean hands, and hair combed. In other respects they
were to come as their circumstances would admit.'[24]

An anecdote about Raikes' practice of visiting poor families
showed either his willingness to humiliate himself to achieve his
purpose or his fondness of histrionics. On one occasion he is said
to have called at the home of a 'poor, but respectable' woman,
whose little girl was causing her considerable trouble and distress
because of her 'exceeding bad temper'. The mother told Raikes
'that she had done all she could to correct her', but to no avail.
With her mother's consent Raikes tried reasoning with the sulky
girl and suggested, very seriously, that she should kneel down
and ask her mother's forgiveness, but without effect. 'At last he
said, "Well then, if you have no regard for yourself, I must have
regard for you: you will be ruined and lost if you do not begin at
once to be a good girl; and if you do not humble yourself, I must
humble myself, amd make a beginning for you." He then kneeled
down before the child's mother, and putting his hands together
like a penitent offender, asked her forgiveness. No sooner did the
stubborn girl see him on his knees on her account, than her pride
yielded; her obstinacy was overcome; she burst into tears; fell
upon her knees; earnestly entreated her mother's forgiveness;
and from that hour conducted herself as an obedient and gentle
child.'[25]

Raikes meant every word when he said that his school was 'cal-

culated to admit the poorest and most neglected'. Children were
not refused admission because of their dirty or ragged clothes or
their lack of discipline. Raikes exhorted his scholars, 'If you have
no clean shirt, come in that you have on . . . if you can loiter
about without shoes, and in a ragged coat, you may as well come
to school, and learn what may tend to your good in that garb.'[26]
Several more or less contemporary accounts of the sort of children
attending Raikes' Sunday schools confirm his descriptions of
them as the poorest and most neglected. Mrs Caroline Watkins,
the granddaughter of Mrs Critchley, said of Raikes' Sunday
school in Southgate Street, 'The children who were brought there
were the very lowest kind that could be found,'[27] and her
brother, John Oakley Packer, Registrar of Births and Deaths and
sexton of St Mary de Crypt Church, made the comment about the
boys attending his grandmother's Sunday school, 'a rough lot
they were by all accounts'.[28] William Brick, who had been a scholar at Raikes' Sunday school in 1807 contended, 'Some turrible
chaps went to the school when I first went . . . (and) there were
always bad 'uns coming in.'[29] A former Sunday school scholar
named Bourne described an incident he remembered which took
place in 1800, 'The first Sunday school I went (to) a boy called
"Winkin' Jim" brought a young badger with him and turned it
loose. You should have seen old Mother Critchley jump! I laugh
now! I shall never forget my first Sunday, nor Winkin Jim. He
went to sea, and was rolled off the yard and drowned.'[30] An old
man of eighty named Cooksey recalled in 1863 that when he went
to Mrs Critchley's school, 'The boys would play tricks on each
other and begin to fight in no time.'[31] Old Sunday school scholars
have alleged that the attendance of some boys was secured only
with great difficulty, although Raikes, at the age of seventy-two,
was said to have denied this. William Brick averred, 'I know the
parents of one or two of them used to walk them to school with
14lb weights tied to their legs,' and he continued, 'sometimes
boys would be sent to school with logs of wood tied to their ank-
les, just as though they were wild jackasses, which I suppose
they were, only worse.'[32] An old man, Samuel Pitt of Green
Court, King's Stanley, near Stroud, in 1863 stated that he had
heard stories of boys being 'strapped' all the way to school by
their parents and when asked what was meant by being strapped
replied, 'The men used to wear leather belts, and when they took

them off and laid them on the youngsters that was "belting" or "strapping" . . . No one would take any notice of boys being punished in Sunday schools when they first started, or during Mr. Raikes' lifetime. The only sense you could appeal to in the boys who were first got together was the sense of pain; I am sure of that. Some of 'em were so hard, it was difficult to find where they felt.'[33]

The children admitted were between five and fourteen years of age. 'Boys and girls above this age, who have been totally undisciplined,' wrote Raikes, 'are generally too refractory for this government.'[34] The teachers had charge of a class of approximately twenty children, the boys and girls being taught separately. Each class was divided by the teacher into four groups with a monitor, usually the 'best' boy or girl in the group acting as its leader. The monitors, having been instructed by the teachers, undertook some of the teaching and supervision, such as helping children to practise their spelling.

Times of attendance appear to have varied from one school to another. Raikes said of the agreement he made with the first four teachers employed, 'The children were to come soon after ten in the morning and stay until twelve: they were then to go home and return at one, and after a reading lesson they were to be conducted to church. After church they were to be employed in repeating the catechism till half after five, and then to be dismissed, with the injunction to go home without making a noise, and by no means to play in the streets.'[35] Stock envisaged schools opening at eight o'clock in the morning, although in practice it was usually half past eight before the school commenced, because he wanted the children to attend church both in the morning and the afternoon.[36] Miss Priscilla Kirby, interviewed in 1863, when she was seventy-five, described Mrs Bretherton's Sunday school in Hare Lane which she attended, 'The children used to go to school at ten o'clock on a Sunday morning. We used to go to school in the church in the afternoon, and after service in the afternoon Mr. Stock used to come to us. He used to explain the Scriptures to us. We used to learn reading Catechisms and Answers – Mann's Catechism and Lewis's, I think. He used to stay until twelve o'clock. We went again at two o'clock in the afternoon, and every third Sunday Mr. Stock used to address us in public in the church.'[37] A Mrs Summerill, one of Raikes' scho-

lars, still living in Gloucester in 1880, said, 'We went to school at
nine o'clock every Sunday morning. About fifty boys and fifty
girls attended. Our bonnets and tippets were taken off when we
went to school, and others of white linen given us. We had to
wear those till the afternoon so that we were obliged to come to
afternoon school to get back our own. After school we were taken
to church, which was over about 12.30. We went to church again
at 3 and after church had school till 6.'[38]

Another advantage Raikes had as founder of Sunday schools
was his ready access to published works. The provision of
equipment for the Sunday schools presented no difficulty to
Raikes: primer readers, spelling books, catechisms, testaments,
hymnals, and religious and morally instructive literature were
readily obtainable through his business connections. As early as
1758, during twelve months of his editorship, he advertised and
sold 'in short sections priced 3d at the printing office . . . a new
copy of the HOLY BIBLE, both Old and New Testaments, Illustrated with Notes and Explications, which explain the difficult
Passages therein (and) unfold Sublime truths they teach.' George
II had granted 'his Royal Letter of Licence for' this work 'in consideration of the use which it might be of'. Also in the same year
Raikes advertised and sold, 'A new and easy spelling book for
children, priced 6d, being well adapted to their tender capacities,
as to render it a more useful Book for Ease and speedy instruction
of children, than any of the Kind and Price extant. Part I consisting of tables of Two, Three, Four, Five, Six and Seven Letters
with easy and instructive lessons after each Table. Part II (containing) Alphabetical Tables of Two, Three, and Four Syllables: with
easy and instructive lessons after each, and not exceeding the
Number of Syllables of the preceding Tables; also the Church
Catechism broke into short Questions: likewise short and easy
Prayers for Morning and Evening: Graces before and after Meat,
Divine Songs and Hymns, Fables and several other necessary and
useful things.'

In 1780 Raikes' *Journal* carried advertisements for three new
works, all of which could have proved useful to Sunday school
teachers and scholars. The importance with which the first book
was regarded is evident in the advertisement.
'Gloucester Journal, 13th March.
By the King's (George III's) Authority This day was published

Necessary for all Families A New Edition of the New Whole Duty of Man containing the Faith as well as Practice of a Christian made easy for the Practice of the Present Age, as the Old Whole Duty of Man was designed for those unhappy Times in which it was written and supplying the Articles of the Christian Faith.

This Whole Duty of Man printed in Octavo is priced 5s., in large twelves 3s 6d, and in small twelves 2s 6d and sold with the same Allowance as the Old Whole Duty of Man was to those Gentlemen and Ladies who, out of a tender Regard to promote the eternal welfare of their poor and Uninstructed Neighbours and Servants are disposed to give them away.'

On the 6th May was issued, price 6d, the first of a hundred weekly parts of the 'Royal Universal Public Bible – a complete Library of Divine Knowledge containing the Sacred Texts of the Old and New Testaments, with Apocrypha at large: illustrated Notes, Critical, Historical, Theological, and Practical.'

The advertisement for the third work appeared in the *Gloucester Journal* on Monday, 24 July. 'THE CHILD'S best INSTRUCTOR in SPELLING & READING by John Entick, M.A. in which the division of Syllables is taught in such a Natural Way that the learner may soon attain a Pronunciation of Words, which is not acquired by any other method.'

In 1785, a little book, printed by Raikes, was in use in the Sunday schools. The full title of the 1794 edition gives us an idea of its contents. *The Sunday Scholar's Companion; Consisting of Scripture Sentences, disposed in such order, As will quickly ground Young Learners in the Fundamental Doctrines of our most Holy Religion; And at the same time Lead them Pleasantly on from Simple and Easy to Compound and Difficult Words.*[39]

After the initial experiments, the setting up of the Sunday schools proved straightforward. Teachers, willing to accept the strain of such formidable work, were engaged; suitable premises to be adapted as schoolrooms were found, and the equipping of the schools was relatively easy. The major challenge for the founders was their personal involvement in a turmoil of complex human relationships. As we have seen Raikes collected together all the 'worst cases' he could find: the most difficult, neglected, deprived, ill-used children. To have permanently modified and civilised the behaviour of some of the early Sunday school scholars would have called for highly developed psychological, perhaps psychiatric, techniques. Raikes could only experiment and learn by trial and error. In his own words he was 'botanising in human nature'.[40] Both Stock and Raikes realised that the Sunday schools required supervision and leadership and the disciplinary function of the school was regarded as most important. The rules for the conduct of the children were drawn up by Mr Stock. 'Mr. Stock was a great disciplinarian,' said Miss Kirby, for ten years mistress of Hare Lane Sunday school, and she added with respect and affection, 'I profited very much under him. He did me good. He gave me kind instruction and sound advice.'[41]

Raikes' relationship with the children was, for the most part, friendly, gracious, gentle, kindly and benevolent, and as a newspaperman who liked imparting information to his readers, he enjoyed telling children interesting things. Raikes discerned what every teacher knows: that without order little progress will be made, and that to a large extent order depends upon the personality of the teacher. The rules and regulations compiled by Stock would help in the establishment of routines, timing, and determining strategies, but the choice of teachers would be critical for the carrying out of the aims of the founders. Raikes saw to it that, in the schools he supervised, a hierarchy of authorities was acknowledged by the children. He himself became a symbol of authority: he showed all the confidence of a successful businessman, his appearance was striking, his dress attractive, his purpose definite. It seems unlikely that he ever showed embarrassment, timidity or indecision. He was a man of conviction and the parents, teachers and children knew him to be sincere, dedicated and determined.

His Sunday school scholars appreciated his interest in them as individuals and he impressed them with his judicious praise. Miss Ann Hannam, when a seventy-three year old inmate of the old women's day ward of the Gloucester Union, a workhouse for the destitute poor and aged, in 1863, could still remember Raikes: 'He had a very good way with children . . . He had authority with him and yet they were not afraid; and he would pat them on the head and on cheeks, and touch them under the chin and say they were good and nice and clean, if they were so. He liked to see boys' and girls' hair combed. Many children never saw a comb before he gave them one. Their hair was all matted, and it was not easy to use a comb at first. The children would use their fingers for a time.'[42] Mr Eycott, a sixty-one year old furniture broker of Gloucester, who alleged that he was six or seven years old when he first went to Raikes' Sunday school, recalled that, 'Robert Raikes had a knack of touching the boys under their chins and saying: "That is a nice little boy." He used to take us sometimes into his garden, and whoever was the best boy in his examining of us, was the best rewarded by him.'[43] Rewards and punishments were major incentives in Raikes' Sunday schools. Mrs Caroline Watkins, Mrs Critchley's granddaughter, was certain that 'Some (children) were induced to come by promises of nice things to be given them if they would come regularly, and wash themselves and comb their hair tidy.'[44] Miss Priscilla Kirby, the seventy-five year old former teacher, already quoted, said that 'Mr. Robert Raikes and his brother, the Rev. Richard Raikes, used to come occasionally to visit us, and see how we progressed: he (Robert Raikes) used to distribute a crown in small prizes.'[45] Raikes himself wrote, 'To those children who distinguish themselves as examples of diligence, quietness of behaviour, observance of order, kindness to their companions, etc., etc., I give some little token of my regard, as a pair of shoes if they are barefooted, and some who are very bare of apparel I clothe.'[46] Mrs Summerill, a former pupil, already quoted, recalled that 'After morning church Mr. Raikes used to hear us all say the Collect for the day in church, and whoever said it best had a penny. Mr. Raikes was always at church himself. In school the Bible and Catechism were taught us. Tickets were given for rewards, and for a certain number of tickets a Prayer book. I remember having one with red covers.'[47]

Raikes has left us a picture of the kind of disciplinarian that he would have liked to have been. He wrote, 'I have often, too, the satisfaction of receiving thanks from parents, for the reformation they perceive in their children. Often I have given them kind admonitions, which I always do in the mildest and gentlest manner. The going among them, doing them little kindnesses, distributing trifling rewards, and ingratiating myself with them, I hear, has given me an ascendency, greater than I ever could have imagined: for I am told by their mistresses that they are very much afraid of my displeasure.'[48]

Another side of Raikes was seen, however, which was neither gentle nor kind. There are accounts of punishments, administered by him or carried out at his instigation, which were unjustifiably harsh. Although only three witnesses give evidence of this, there seemed no reason for them to make misleading or false statements. William Brick declared, 'I can remember Mr. Raikes well enough. I remember his caning me. I don't suppose I minded it much. He used to cane boys on the back of a chair.'[49] Raikes seems to have acted with strong determination in the correction of miscreants, even demanding the participation of a child's parents in using corporal punishment. 'When a boy was very bad,' continued Brick, 'he (Mr. Raikes) would take him out of the school and march him home and get his parents to "wallop" him. He'd stop and see it done, and then bring the young urchin back, rubbing his eyes and other places. Mr. Raikes was a terror to all evil doers and a praise to them that did well. Everyone in the city loved and feared him.'[50]

Some of the disciplinary measures taken by Raikes, if a second witness, the old Sunday school scholar, Bourne, is to be believed, were extremely drastic. 'Mr. Raikes used always to come to school on Sundays and inquire what the children had learnt, and whether they had been "good boys." If there had been extra bad boys, or Mrs. Critchley was out of temper and put it on strong, then he would punish them himself.' Raikes carried out the punishment, Bourne averred, 'The same way as boys were birched. An old chair was the birching stool or horse. The chair was laid on its two front legs downwards, and then the young 'un was put on, kicking and swearing all the time, if he were pretty big and pretty new. Then Mr. Raikes would cane him. I knew a boy he could never draw a tear from – we used to say he couldn't feel. I don't know whether he could or no. One boy was a notorious liar. No, I don't remember his name for certain. He was sure to have a nickname, but I don't remember it. Mr. Raikes could do nothing with him, and one day he caught him by the hand and pressed the tips of his fingers on the bars of the stove or fireplace.' When asked if the boy was burnt Bourne replied, 'Blistered a bit. Mr. Raikes would take care that he was not much injured; but he did hate liars! Look at my book. This is what he printed for us to learn: "A thief is better than a man who is accustomed to lie . . ."'[51] Samuel Pitt, the third witness, had heard of Raikes chastising children and recalled a conversation Mrs Critchley had with his aunt. 'I have heard her speak in word of praise of

Mr. Raikes, but the boys were sometimes too much even for his temper.'[52]

Our knowledge of Raikes as a teacher, although chiefly anecdotal, and written by himself, indicates his sense of fun, the depth of his religious feeling, and the joy he experienced in promoting the happiness of children. He wrote in 1793, 'I have lately had a new flock of children come about me from a singular circumstance. I was shewing my Sunday scholars a little time ago how possible it is for an invisible power to exist in Bodies which shall act upon other Bodies without our being able to perceive in what manner they act. This I prove to them by the powers of the Magnet. They see the magnet draw the Needle without touching it. Thus, I tell them, I wish to draw them to the paths of duty, and thus lead them to Heaven and Happiness; and as they saw one Needle, when it touched the Magnet, then capable of drawing another Needle, thus when they became good, they would be made the instruments in the hands of God, very probably, of making other boys good. Upon this idea those children are now endeavouring to bring other children to meet me at Church, and you would be diverted to see with what a groupe I am surrounded every morning at seven o'clock prayers at the Cathedral, especially upon a Sunday morning, at which time I give Books, or Combs, or other encouragements.

'Sometimes they read me a part of the Gospel for the Day, which I explain in a manner suited and applied to their own situations and comprehensions. They were reading that verse in St. Luke, the other morning, where our Saviour says, "The Kingdom of God cometh not with observation – the Kingdom of God is within you" – "Who can tell me," says I, "what we are to understand by that expression, – The Kingdom of God is within you?" They were all silent for some minutes. At last, the Boy who was reading said, "I believe it means, when the Spirit of God is in our hearts."'[53]

Raikes experienced the delights of teaching children. He wrote, 'My children last Sunday told me they were sorry when the time came that I was to leave them. The Subject of my conversation with them was the History of Joseph. It had occurred in the Lesson of the Day. I brought it down to a level with their condition, representing Joseph as a poor boy, like one of them. You would have been agreeably struck with the fixed attention of their little minds. I daresay many went home and told the story to their parents.'[54] The marvellous sense of wonder of children caused Raikes amusement. 'I had some time ago been exerting my feeble powers to convey some ideas of this kind (going about doing good) to some poor children at the opening of a Sunday school in a village in this Neighbourhood, where 'till then the poor had been entirely neglected: and a little Boy who had listened attentively to my conversation, went home to his Mother (as I was afterwards informed) and asked her, – whether that Gentleman had not been at Heaven?'[55] In another letter Raikes gives us a description of how he endeavoured to 'avail (himself) of the folly of the bad to strengthen the good'. 'In my visit to my Sunday school last Sunday,' he wrote, 'I remarked some of my sheep had gone astray. On my enquiry, one of the Boys told me they were at play with a set of wicked boys in a neighbouring field. "Alas!" said I, "the wicked one was afraid we should lead all the poor boys to Heaven. He has therefore set up a Sunday School against us to lead some of them to his place of Torment. Let those then who take pleasure in wickedness go to their Master, but I know all who wish to call God their Friend, will come and take part with me. But do you now mark the end of these boys who have joined our Adversary, and their Fate, I am convinced, will confirm you in your duty.'"[56] Sunday school 'treats' were times of enjoyment to all. Raikes wrote, 'I have invited all my Sunday School Children to dine with me on New Year's Day on Beef and Plumb Pudding. I wish you could step in and see what clean and joyous countenances we shall exhibit, and you would not be displeased to hear how well they sing their Maker's Praise.'[57]

Pleasure and satisfaction from the work of the Sunday schools was not derived by Raikes alone. The children also remembered equally pleasurable experiences, and an instance of this is found in an anecdote published in 1813, two years after Raikes' death. '"One day," said Mr. Raikes, "as I was going to church, I overtook a soldier just entering the church door; this was on a weekday. As I passed him I said it gave me pleasure to see that he was going to a place of worship. 'Ah! Sir,' replied he, 'I may thank you for that.' 'Me,' said I, 'why? I do not know I ever saw you before.' 'Sir,' replied the soldier, 'when I was a little boy, I was indebted to you for my first instruction in my duty. I used to meet you at the morning service in this Cathedral, and was one of your

Sunday scholars. My father, when he left this city, took me into Berkshire, and put me apprentice to a shoemaker. I used often to think of you. At length I went to London, and was there drawn to serve as a militia-man, in the Westminster militia. I came to Gloucester last night with a deserter, and I took the opportunity this morning to visit the old spot, and in the hope of once more seeing you.' He then told me his name, and brought himself to my recollection by a curious circumstance which happened whilst he was at school. His father was a journeyman currier, a most vile, profligate man. After the boy had been some time at school, he came one day and told me that his father was wonderfully changed; and that he had left off going to the alehouse on a Sunday. It happened soon after that I met the man in the street, and said to him – 'My friend, it gives me great pleasure to hear that you have left off going to the alehouse on the Sunday; your son tells me that you now stay at home, and never get tipsy.' He immediately replied that I had been the means of this change being produced. On my expressing my surprise at this, on account of never having so much as spoken to him before, he replied, 'No, Sir, but the good instruction which you gave my boy at the Sunday school, he repeats to me; and this has so convinced me of the error of my former life as to have led to my present reformation.' '' [58]

The success of the Sunday schools in bringing about changes in the behaviour of children was remarkable and surprising. Raikes' scholars would have proved a challenge to the best-equipped school with the most highly trained and experienced staff. The Sunday school founders and teachers had none of these advantages: they worked under severe limitations, the time available being not the least of these.

The intellectual content of the curriculum, unless catechetical instruction and the memorising of collects, biblical passages, and hymns are adjudged to be 'intellectual', consisted of the teaching of reading and spelling to a very elementary standard. Writing does not appear to have been taught. The former scholar, Bourne, stated definitely, 'No writing was taught in the school in my time,' [59] and Eycott maintained, 'The only education I ever received was at Robert Raikes' school. I cannot write.' [60]

Social training was of special importance. 'The great principle I inculcate,' wrote Raikes, 'is, to be kind and good natured to each other; not to provoke one another; to be dutiful to their parents; not to offend God by cursing and swearing; and such little plain precepts as all may comprehend.'[61] Regular and frequent warnings against cursing and swearing were necessary since bad language amongst the labouring classes, whose vocabulary through lack of education was too inadequate to permit facility of expression, was almost endemic. Discord through high words, wrangles, squabbles, quarrels and fights was settled by sound common-sense approaches and Raikes' own statement contains a sense of achievement. 'The children are frequently admonished to refrain from swearing; and certain boys who are distinguished by their decent behaviour are appointed to superintend the conduct of the rest, and make report of all those that swear, call names etc. When quarrels have arisen, the aggressor is compelled to ask pardon, and the offended is enjoined to forgive. The happiness that must arise to all from a kind, good-natured behaviour is often inculcated. This mode of treatment has produced a wonderful change in the manners of these little savages.'[62] Insistence upon the cleanliness and tidiness in appearance of the children by Raikes, already noted, was confirmed by Miss Arabella Herbert, a seventy-two year old resident of 40 Worcester Street, Gloucester. Miss Herbert, interviewed in 1863, claimed to have known the Sunday school founder well. 'Mr. Raikes used to like to see the girls clean and neat, and bonnets were provided for them on Sundays. This was not done for a long time after the starting of the schools – the girls had to be civilised first. They were worse than the boys, I have heard many people say.'[63] Mrs Caroline Watkins could still remember the rhyme she heard when she was young,

'Clean hands, clean face, and tidy combed hair,
Are better than fine clothes to wear.'[64]

The central characteristic and indispensable heart of the Sunday school was the religious teaching. Changes of a lasting nature in outlook and behaviour of scholars resulted from a sensible understanding of their needs, convincing teaching and noble example. Raikes attempted to make the teaching meaningful and related to the condition of the children. 'Their attending the service of the church once a day has, to me, seemed sufficient,' he explained to a friend in 1787, 'for their time may be spent more profitably, perhaps, in receiving instruction than in being present at a long discourse, which their minds are not yet able to comprehend.'[65] Raikes expressed his message simply, 'It is that part of our Saviour's character which I aim at imitating. He went about doing good.'[66]

The establishment of the original Sunday schools in Gloucester resulted from the close co-operation and joint effort of the two founders. The Revd Thomas Stock, described by G. W. Counsel, one of his personal friends, as 'a man of great literary attainments and most exemplary conduct: and notwithstanding, he made it the business and pleasure of his life to go about doing good by instruction in righteousness and works of charity, yet he never sought the applause of men',[67] took upon himself the inspection of three out of the four Sunday schools, addressed the children and saw the teachers weekly at his house or the Cathedral School when they came for payment. Robert Raikes supervised the fourth school, undertook some of the teaching, visited the other three schools sometimes when the opportunity arose. Both Stock and Raikes led busy lives before undertaking their onerous work with the Sunday schools. Stock managed to visit them frequently before or after his church services and Raikes after he had completed the editing of his paper, which came out on Mondays. Challenging and exhausting though the work undoubtedly was, Raikes, and almost certainly Stock, seem to have enjoyed that enchantment and delight experienced by all who take pleasure in working with children. For the worldly Raikes, perhaps far more than for the godly Stock, the work of the Sunday school as a social disciplinary force was its *sine qua non*. Raikes had seen for himself the cruel realities of life for the poor. To him the Sunday school came to represent a power to reform society.

NOTES

[1] A. P. Wadsworth, *The First Manchester Sunday Schools: Bulletin of the John Rylands Library* No 33 (1951) p 303
[2] Alfred Gregory, *Robert Raikes: Journalist and Philanthropist* (1880) p 53
[3] Raikes, *Letter* 5 June, 1785
[4] A. Platts and G. H. Hainton, *Education in Gloucestershire: A Short History* (1953) p 25
[5] Ibid p 26
[6] M. G. Jones, *The Charity School Movement* (1938) p 47
[7] J. W. Adamson, *A Short History of Education* (1919) pp 198, 199

8 T. Simpson Evans (editor), *The Life of Robert Frampton, Bishop of Gloucester* (1876) p vii

9 Mrs Boevey probably had Joseph Addison (1672–1719) and Sir Richard Steele, the founder of the *Tatler*, amongst her suitors. Steele described her playfully as 'The Perverse Widow' and Addison portrayed her as the distractor of Sir Roger de Coverley.

10 Joseph Stratford, *Robert Raikes and Others: The Founders of Sunday Schools* (1880) p 46

11 Ibid pp 46, 47

12 Ibid p 48

13 Ibid

14 Ibid

15 Ibid p 50

16 P. M. Eastman (editor), *Robert Raikes and Northamptonshire Sunday Schools* (1880) p 45

17 *Gloucester Journal* 15 June, 1778

18 Ibid 16 July, 1787

19 James King is said to have received a Bible, signed by Robert Raikes with the date on the fly-leaf July 1780, in appreciation of his wife's work with children.

20 J. H. Harris (editor), *Robert Raikes: The Man and his Work* p 24

21 Ibid

22 *Gloucester Journal* 9 March, 1789

23 Ibid

24 Raikes, *Letter* 5 June, 1785

25 George Maunder, *Biographical Sketches; Eminent Christian Philanthropists* (1877) p 16

26 Raikes, *Letter* 25 November, 1783

27 Harris, op cit p 22

28 Ibid p 18

29 Ibid p 38

30 Ibid p 40

31 Ibid p 38

32 Ibid

33 Ibid p 40

34 Raikes, *Letter* 25 November, 1783

35 Ibid 5 June, 1785

36 Gregory, op cit p 111

37 Harris, op cit pp 26, 27

38 *Gloucester Journal* 3 July, 1880

39 Harris, op cit p 329

40 Raikes, *Letter* 25 November, 1783

41 Harris, op cit pp 28, 29

42 Ibid pp 32, 33

43 Ibid p 30

44 Ibid p 23

45 Ibid p 27

46 Raikes, *Letter* 5 November, 1787

47 *Gloucester Journal* 3 July, 1880

48 Raikes, *Letter* 25 November, 1783

49 Harris, op cit pp 37, 38

50 Ibid p 38

51 Ibid pp 41, 42

52 Ibid p 39

[53] Raikes, *Letter* 8 November, 1793
[54] Ibid   25 March, 1792
[55] Ibid   16 February, 1792
[56] Ibid   16 May, 1792
[57] Ibid   30 December, 1794
[58] Gregory, op cit pp 126, 127
[59] Harris, op cit p 40
[60] Ibid   p 30
[61] Raikes, *Letter* 25 November, 1783
[62] Gregory, op cit pp 120, 121
[63] Harris, op cit p 17
[64] Ibid   p 23
[65] Raikes, *Letter* 5 November, 1787
[66] Ibid
[67] *Gloucester Journal* 15 May, 1841

Chapter 5
PUBLICIST OF THE MOVEMENT

Raikes was the leading publicist of the Sunday School Movement. He was uniquely situated and admirably equipped for this role: he owned and controlled one of the most effective media of the day, a thriving newspaper with an extensive circulation. He associated with others in his profession, with the well-to-do, and with the clergy, and he had their goodwill. His background knowledge and experience of children, young people and prisoners provided him with strong motivation, but perhaps what was more important he had the ideal personality to be a publicist. He was tough enough to enjoy the limelight.

Raikes' belief in the efficacy of the Sunday school as a religious and social disciplinary force, as well as a means of increasing the well-being of the poor and hence of society, was so absolute that he seems to have used every suitable opportunity to bring others to the same conviction. But Raikes was not tedious: he was perceptive in gauging the reactions of others and could be sufficiently persuasive and subtle in his approach to achieve his own ends. He was very happy to let people build up their own myths about him, eg, if they liked to think he was a paragon, it didn't worry him.

Within his own city of Gloucester, then having a population of under 6,500, it is probable that nearly all the inhabitants knew of Raikes and his Sunday schools. Printer, newspaper editor and proprietor, and a man of substance in the city, local people could hardly avoid recognising his colourful, stylishly dressed, corpulent figure, with his own peculiar gait, accompanying the lines of ragged urchins walking two by two with their Sunday school teachers to church. The group of eager, poorly clothed youngsters who gathered round him outside the Cathedral when he publicly distributed his little gifts of combs, etc, must have occasioned comments from members of the congregation. That tongues should wag was probably precisely what Raikes intended. To him derisory remarks such as 'crank' and scornful

ROBERT RAIKES,

FOUNDER OF SUNDAY SCHOOLS.

BORN, SEPTEMBER XIV., MDCCXXXIV.   DIED, APRIL V., MDCCCXI.

never pass the spot where the word " Try " came so powerfully into my mind, without lifting
my hands and heart to Heaven for having first put such a thought into my heart."

Robert Raikes

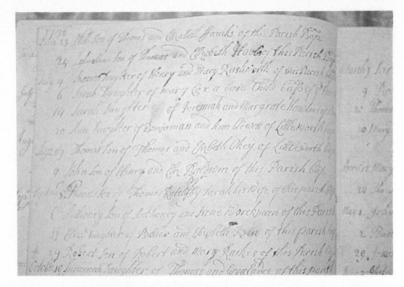

Baptismal register, St Mary de Crypt

Raikes' house in Southgate Street

Plaque in Ashbury Church, Berkshire

The plaque reads:

Be it remembered that in the chancel of this church the Reverend Thomas Stock, curate of this parish, in the year 1777 opened a Sunday school. This later became the first of its kind in England to be housed outside the church in a building of its own: still to be seen near the present church school.

The Revd Thomas Stock

THOMAS STOCK.

The portrait of Mr Stock is taken, by permission, from a sketch made by Robert Dowling, Esq., for the "Origin of Sunday Schools."

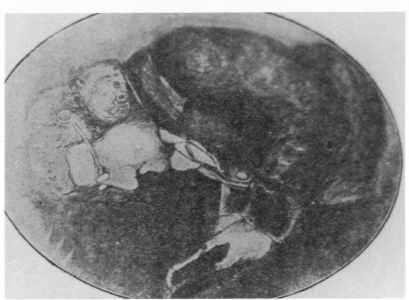

William King of Dursley

William Fox

Gloucester Castle Gaol, pulled down about 1786

New County Gaol, Gloucester

A typical street scene in Gloucester about 1780

Raikes with children in one of his Sunday schools

School for girls, 1780

Early Sunday schools in Gloucester

House of James King, Catherine Street

nicknames like 'Bobby Wildgoose' would mean that Sunday schools were a topic of conversation and therefore gaining useful publicity. The more they were discussed the sooner the aims of the founders would come to be appreciated. By being seen with the Sunday school children Raikes added the weight of his approbation, authority and status to the Sunday schools and gave a lead to others more reserved or reluctant to help.

Through an anecdote told by C. H. Wilton, a young student of Raikes' acquaintance, we learn that the printer had the scholars of his Sunday school, probably those taught by Mrs Critchley, assemble and be seated in his garden, with the specific intention that they should be seen, and possibly their singing heard, by his guests. On the occasion described Raikes received a critical, unexpected response from one of these guests. 'Mr Raikes invited some friends to breakfast; the window of the room opened into a small garden, which was a rising ground, and there on seats, one row above another, sat the first Sunday school, neatly dressed. They were purposely exhibited to the breakfast party, to interest them in the design; but so little were the momentous consequences then appreciated, that a Quaker lady rebuked Mr Raikes in these words: "Friend Raikes, when thou doest charitably, thy right hand should not know what thy left hand doeth."'[1] We are not told of Raikes' reply, but it is doubtful whether he would have been abashed.

As one who personally visited the homes of poor families to persuade parents to send their children to Sunday school, Raikes probably prepared and printed leaflets which might be left, or delivered by children, for those parents who could read, or who might have them read to them. One such leaflet entitled, *A Plain and Serious Address to Parents of Poor Children on the Subject of Sunday Schools*, was the work of a single writer, who might have been Raikes. The reader is informed of the good intentions of the Sunday school founders and assured that the children's attendance at Sunday school is without cost to the parents. All that is required is stated clearly in the opening paragraph.

'My Christian Friends,

Permit one, who wishes well to you and your children, to address you on the subject of Sunday Schools. Many thoughtful and serious Christians, grieved at the profligacy which too much prevails among the lower class of people, and persuaded that this arises in a great measure from ignorance and the profanation of the Sabbath, have set up these Schools, that your children might be instructed in their duty towards God and man. But unless you do something on your part, they have reason to fear that their endeavours will not be attended with that success they wish for. They do not require you to contribute any thing of what you gain by your daily labour: They cheerfully provide all that is necessary for the instruction of your children. What they desire of you is this, to take care that they shall partake of this instruction, by attending regularly, and going to school in proper time: and they further wish, that you would ask them what they have learned, and set them good examples.'

Eight questions to parents (abbreviated here), indicating aims of the Sunday schools, follow the salutation and first paragraph. 'Do you think it best to have your children playing about on a Sunday, wandering you know not where, and, for aught you can tell, in the worst of company? Do you think it best for them to be orderly and decent in their behaviour, or grow up in a rude, uncivilised state? Is it not right that God should be worshipped by his reasonable creatures? Is it desirable that your children should learn to read the word of God? Do you wish to have your children dutiful or undutiful? Is it your wish that your children may prove sober and industrious? Do you believe your children must be happy or miserable in another world? (Surely you know that the wicked shall be punished with everlasting destruction, and the righteous rewarded with everlasting happiness.) Do you believe that you are accountable to God for the instruction of your children?'

In the final paragraphs the writer requested parents solemnly to consider what might happen 'on the day of Judgement'. Would their children make the accusation, 'O cruel parents, you neglected to instruct us, and neglected to send us where we might have been instructed. We were young and thoughtless, and not aware of the advantage of spending the Sabbath in a proper manner, but you might have known it. It is in part through your neglect that we are unfit for happiness in heaven, and fit only for the regions of darkness and despair.' Alternatively, it was argued, had the parents taken care that their children attended Sunday school regularly, and especially if they had endeavoured 'to instruct them at home', and 'set before them good examples', then they may hope 'through the blessing of God' that their children 'will prove comforts' to them and feel great joy 'from seeing them fill up their stations in life with the usefulness and honour, which they may do whatever those stations are'. Then the parents were assured that they would say, 'Blessed be God, who put it into the hearts of his servants to establish Sunday Schools. We see and feel the happy effects of them. By hearing our children repeating their catechism and hymns, our attention is called to God, and to our duty. Thus both we and they are become better.'

Raikes, the publicist, presumably for the benefit of other Sunday school founders who might wish to produce something similar, as well as for the interest of his readers, printed in full in the *Gloucester Journal* an admonitory address of 20 March, 1786, which had been written by the Revd W. D. Tattersall, pastor of the small Gloucestershire town of Wotton-under-Edge, and distributed among the poor parents of his parish. This 'worthy' cleric, of whom it was said, 'few men (had) entered upon the work of civilisation with more zeal and judgement', assembled 'the children of the poor to a number of between two and three hundred at school every Sunday morning, and brought (them) to public worship'.

'To the poor Inhabitants of the parish of Wotton-under-Edge, in the county of Gloucester. As two SUNDAY SCHOOLS are established for the benefit and instruction of your children, let me earnestly recommend it to you to avail yourselves of the advantages which this Institution offers, and which your benefactors wish and desire, that you should reap from it.

'It is your duty, not only to provide food and raiment, and other necessaries of life, for those you have brought into the world; but it is equally incumbent upon you to train them up for a better and a happier state, by impressing on their tender minds notions of God and religion; and endeavouring to make them useful members of society.

'With this view let me intreat you to send them regularly to school on the Lord's day, that they may not only be kept from spending the day in a loose and idle manner, but be taught a decent orderly behaviour, and be instructed in their duty both to God and man, and in the knowledge of the Holy Scriptures, which alone are able to make them wise unto Salvation.

'But above all, be ye yourselves careful to set a good example. This is a matter of the utmost consequence, as your children will be naturally inclined to imitate you in their lives and conversation. Let me therefore pray you on this account to avoid drunkenness, profane cursing and swearing, Sabbath breaking and the like; if you are guilty of these vices, it may have a most unhappy influence on your children, and may lead them in the end to the worst and most abandoned villainies.' The three concluding paragraphs of the admonition warned the readers that 'it is a fearful thing for the sinner to fall into the hands of the living God', and called for them to 'repent, and amend, and walk in the paths of piety and virtue'.[2]

Raikes' first announcement in respect of Sunday schools appeared in the *Gloucester Journal* on 3 November, 1783.

'Some of the clergy in different parts of this county, bent upon attempting a reform among the children of the lower class, are establishing Sunday Schools, for rendering the Lord's Day subservient to the ends of instruction, which has hitherto been prostituted to bad purposes. Farmers and other inhabitants of the towns and villages, complain that they receive more injury in their property on the Sabbath, than all the week besides: This in great measure proceeds from the lawless state of the younger class, who are allowed to run wild, on that day, free from every restraint. To remedy this evil, persons duly qualified are employed to instruct those that cannot read, and those that may have learnt to read, are taught the catechism, and conducted to church. By thus keeping their minds engaged, the day passes profitably and not disagreeably. – In those parishes where this plan has been adopted, we are assured, that the behaviour of the children is greatly civilised. The barbarous ignorance, in which they had before lived, being in some degree dispelled; they begin to give proofs that those persons are mistaken, who consider the lower orders of mankind as incapable of improvement, and therefore think an attempt to reclaim them impracticable, or at least not worth the trouble.'

Raikes gave all the credit to the clergy although he knew also of lay people, beside himself, who had founded Sunday schools. The instruction of the poor, particularly the children, he considered (as he is purported to have said to William King – see page 65), was the holy trust of the Church and the duty of the clergy.

Raikes hoped that justification for the establishment of Sunday schools would have wide appeal. He mentioned 'Farmers' in particular, because as the country was chiefly agricultural, clergy in many parishes would need their support. Raikes' publicity of the effectiveness of Sunday schools in changing the behaviour of poor children undoubtedly contributed to the rapid and extensive growth of Sunday schools. In fact the Sunday School Movement, as such, started from this first cleverly written reference to them.

Raikes' concluding sentence was of tremendous importance to the whole nation. It was gently persuasive. Many influential people, probably a majority of the ruling class, regarded the poor as hopelessly ignorant, ineducable, and absolutely beyond redemption. Raikes had answered subtly and astutely, in the affirmative, the very crucial question of whether the nation could or should teach all of its children. Little wonder that Raikes' announcement of 3 November, 1783 was later printed in the London papers!

He argued from the conviction of several years' personal experience of Sunday schools, his own and those of others. Raikes was said to have received information from the Revd John Marks Moffatt about his Sunday School at Forest Green Chapel, Nailsworth, already mentioned.

Another Sunday school founder at this time was Sophia Cooke, daughter of John Cooke, surgeon, a native of Gloucester. Miss Cooke established a Sunday school in 1777 in a house in a squalid part of the city, called 'Pye Corner'.[3] Here, assisted by her sister, she taught some of the children who worked in the pin factory of one Alderman Weaver, an uncle of the sisters. Later Sophia married the Revd Samuel Bradburn, a Methodist, and became a great friend of John Wesley. Her nephew, Charles Cooke, surgeon, of Cambray Terrace, Cheltenham, is alleged to have had in his possession a manuscript which showed that his aunt, Sophia Cooke, had been personally acquainted with Raikes and had suggested to him a plan of Sunday school instruction for the large number of ragged children whom they saw in the streets of Gloucester. Raikes had agreed to help teach poor neglected children to read and to take them to church. It was 'Mr Raikes and Miss Cooke', contended the writer of the manuscript, who 'conducted the first company of Sunday scholars' to church and were 'exposed to public laughter as they passed along the streets with their unpromising charges'.[4] This has not been further verified, but it seems certain that Miss Cooke set up a Sunday school and that Raikes had knowledge of it.

A third Sunday school known to Raikes was kept by one William Twining, a cloth weaver. Samuel Webb, a wealthy benevolent man, said to be of handsome countenance and genial manners, paid Twining to hold a Sunday school in the kitchen of his house in Rutchill Bottom, Sheepscombe, a hamlet in Painswick, near Gloucester. In certain ways Webb was reminiscent of Raikes. Webb wore 'elegant dress . . . gold buttons on his blue coat, (and) beautiful lace about his waistcoat and cuffs', and he attracted attention by carrying a large green umbrella. He took an interest in children, and enjoyed rewarding them for their behaviour – 'the good had two pence and the bad one penny'.[5] Raikes and Webb went together to visit William Twining's Sunday school, and later, in 1784, Webb established another Sunday school in Painswick, which was greatly publicised by Raikes as a showpiece. The Sunday schools of the Revd J. M. Moffatt, Sophia Cooke, and William Twining all ante-dated those set up by Raikes and Stock in Gloucester in 1780.

Raikes publicised the work being done in Gloucester, although his personal involvement was never mentioned. Six months after his first announcement on Sunday schools, in the *Gloucester Journal* 24 May, 1784, he re-emphasised the points made as he described the effectiveness of the teaching. 'The good effects of the Sunday Schools established in this city, are instanced in the account given by principal persons in the pin, and sack manufactories. Great reformation has taken place among the multitudes whom they employ. From being idle, ungovernable, profligate, and filthy in extreme, they say, the boys and girls are become not only more cleanly and decent in their appearance, but are greatly humanised in their manners, more orderly, tractable, and attentive to business; and of course more serviceable than ever they expected to find them. Cursing and swearing, and other vile expressions, which used to form the sum of their conversation, are now very rarely heard among them. Such, we are assured, is the fact.'

From the initial spark generated by Raikes, the enthusiasm for establishing Sunday schools spread like wildfire. His accounts of Sunday schools were copied into other newspapers in the same way that accounts from other newspapers were inserted in the *Gloucester Journal*. In the years 1784, 1785, and 1786 we can read of schools being established in towns and cities throughout the kingdom. On 24 May, 1784, he reported, 'The London Chronicle of last Tuesday mentions, that the plan of Sunday Schools is taken up with such general concurrence at Leeds, in Yorkshire, that the spirited inhabitants of that place . . . have already admitted near 2,000 poor children' and in October the same year he showed the growth of a movement to establish Sunday schools in a convincing, if quaintly expressed, argument: 'The subscriptions at Derby for the support of Sunday-Schools amount to £186 18s 6d. At Birmingham, Manchester, Sheffield and other manufacturing towns, the subscriptions have been even greater. In so useful a point of view appears this simple plan for attempting some reform in the rising generation of the common people, whose morals at present every considerate person must deplore.'[6]

Raikes himself gave publicity to the establishment of Sunday schools in Gloucestershire and the neighbouring counties. In February, 1784, he wrote that the 'worthy clergyman' of Hempstead, a parish two miles south of Gloucester, had founded a Sunday school 'for receiving all the poor children, where they are not only kept from acts of mischief and roguery on that day, but their time is employed in learning their catechism, and being taught how to read'.[7]

The Sunday school was presented by Raikes as being a panacea for social ills. Depression in the clothing industry caused unemployment among the poor of Minchinhampton, a small Gloucestershire town, where families were left without any other means of subsistence save the poor rate. Some were even driven to abandoning their children who were observed 'idling in the streets and under hedges, perishing with nakedness and hunger'.[8] At the beginning of the winter subscriptions were made and a fund started for the relief of the poor. The Revd P. M. Cornwall preached a charity sermon for 'the Benefit of (the) two Thousand two Hundred distressed, starving and destitute poor' of Minchinhampton, which was later published by Raikes. The money from the sale of the printed copies of the sermon 'it had been agreed unanimously' was to be used for the purchase of flax, which the children of Minchinhampton could be employed in spinning.[9] In February of that year Raikes paid tribute to the judgement, good sense and humanity of those who administered the relief fund for the poor. They had arranged for the men to be employed repairing the highways, and had assembled women and children in the Market House, Minchinhampton, which had been made 'warm and comfortable' and 'there they (were) spinning and carding, more cheerful and happy than ever before'. Those provided with employment were required to attend 'Divine Worship' and Raikes, in his report, offered the suggestion that 'if to this could be added the establishment of Sunday schools for throwing a little knowledge of their duty into the minds of the children, the community might possibly be benefited; at least it will be generally allowed, no harm could be done, in making an experiment of its utility.'[10]

Subsequently a Sunday school was founded in Minchinhampton and later in the year Raikes published a full description of the provision made. 'The children . . . were assembled (daily) and kept at work from six in the morning till eight in the evening, under the care of persons qualified to teach them to spin. – Their earnings have in great measure been sufficient for their support ever since. – Weavers have been constantly kept in full employ to make linen for their shirts and shifts, as well as woollen and linsey woolsey cloth; by which means these poor creatures who before were naked, have received cloaths, also shoes and stockings, under these stipulations; that they regularly attend divine service on the Sunday, and that the children be present at the Sunday-Schools, with their hands and face clean and hair combed, at eight in the morning and at five in the afternoon. Masters and mistresses are appointed to instruct them, and to conduct them to the church, where the curate, who has taken great pains in this good work, catechises them, and rewards those that improve with a bible or testament: – Their names are regularly called over, and those that absent themselves are punished by the forfeiture of their cloaths, which are immediately bestowed upon others. – The reformation effected by this simple, this most practicable scheme, would give delight to every benevolent mind, could they see between two and three hundred children, who were lately from their ignorance and profligacy a disgrace to the country, and a nuisance to the neighbourhood, now become cleanly in their persons, quiet and orderly in their behaviour, and attending the worship of their Creator like rational beings, in which rank they were scarcely to be considered heretofore.'[11]

A few days after the publication of this account Raikes received a letter – an extract from which he inserted in the next edition of his newspaper – confirming the accuracy of his account and informing readers that a similar idea was being pursued at Tetbury, a small town seven miles from Minchinhampton. Raikes' correspondent observed, 'I was last Sunday at Minchinhampton, and was highly pleased to observe that the streets of that town, which, on this day especially, used to be filled with half starved naked little objects, playing and lying about like so many brutes, were now entirely free from them. I enquired how they had been disposed of, and was desired to satisfy myself by taking a view of the Sunday Schools, where I found 300 of these poor creatures sitting in great order, and engaged, some in learning their letters, others spelling, others reading the Testament, &c. The silence and good order that prevailed, astonished me. They all seemed happy and contented. Of the number assembled, I remarked 275, whom the benevolent people of the parish had decently cloathed. What an honour to themselves and to their country! – I have great pleasure in acquainting you, that the spirited inhabitants of Tetbury have begun a very liberal subscription for establishing a similar institution here, and under the guidance of our worthy minister, we seem determined to follow an example, which promises great and permanent benefits to the rising generation of those, whom form the bulk of the people.'[12]

The establishment of Sunday schools proceeded rapidly in Gloucestershire. The next month Raikes received a letter from one of his readers at Tetbury, a market town ten miles south-west of Cirencester, in which it was stated 'Five (Sunday) schools are already opened, to which 77 boys and 88 girls have been admitted.' Included with the letter was a copy of resolutions adopted, with the explanation that as the inhabitants of Tetbury had 'heard of the beneficial effects arising among the children of the poor, in many places, from the establishment of Sunday Schools' it was thought that 'the method they (had) pursued may serve as an outline to other places, which may chuse to enter upon the same measure'.

Raikes, of course, published the resolutions in their entirety. These were set out in a very businesslike way and provide us with the earliest detailed information we have of the management of Sunday schools. Notice had been given in church on Sunday of a meeting to be held 'at the vestry table' to 'nominate persons to form a Committee for managing the Sunday Schools'. The Revd Dr Wickes, Messrs Thomas Wight, Samuel White, Robert Clark (Treasurer) and Richard Cooper were duly appointed and a list of sixteen 'rules and orders' approved. These dealt with general management and day to day conduct; accommodation and heating, teachers' salaries and books, scholars' age of admission, segregation of the sexes, examination of the school by visitors and reports to the committee of subscribers. Four rules reflect well the aims of the founders. 'V That no children be admitted who are under five years of age, and none be excluded because of riper age, but rather have the preference. VI that nothing whatever be taught in the schools, but what is suited immediately to the design of the sabbath, and preserving young people from idleness, immorality and ignorance. VII That the committee have a power to fix a salary for the teachers, provide proper books for the scholars; and that they grant such rewards to the diligent and orderly, as to them shall seem useful and of general advantage. XIII That four quarterly meetings of all benefactors of at least half-a-guinea each, be held in the year.'[13]

Sermons were preached in various churches and later published and the money from the collection in church and the sale of the printed copies was devoted to the establishment and support of Sunday schools. The Sunday schools of Stroud were early examples of those receiving such support. The Revd W. Ellis, Curate of Stroud Parish Church and Chaplain to Lord Ducie, preached a sermon on 29 July, 1784, which Raikes later printed, together with the 'Rules for the MANAGEMENT of the SUNDAY SCHOOLS established in that parish.' The churchwardens and principal inhabitants of the parish of Bisley, a Gloucestershire village near Stroud, requested that a sermon be preached for the benefit of their Sunday schools and Raikes informed his readers that on Sunday, 2 January, 1785, 'A collection was made at the church door to which the parishioners very liberally contributed. Their benevolence was more particularly excited by the proofs they receive that this simple mode of cultivating the morals of the rising generation has already produced an extraordinary alteration in the children; who, from being savage and filthy in their manners and appearance are now become decent, orderly, and

attentive to cleanliness.'[14] In a very short time these Bisley Sunday schools appear to have gained strength both in the number of
children in attendance and in their influence on the adult poor.
Raikes published an extract of a letter from a Gentleman at Bisley
dated 2 March, 1786. 'On Sunday last a charity sermon was
preached in our parish church on behalf of the Sunday Schools
established here. It was a pleasing sight. Three hundred boys
were present. Of this number, forty, who had distinguished
themselves by their quiet, orderly, and diligent deportment, were
new cloathed. – The congregation, which upon this occasion
amounted to 1500 persons, witnessed with pleasure the respectful
silence observed during the service, by the children and their parents, who never were seen in a church before this plan took
place.'[15]

'Charity begins at home', was Raikes' forthright comment in
April, 1785, when Professor White in an additional discourse
included in the new edition of the 'admired sermon . . . preached
before the University of Oxford' stressed 'the duty of attempting
the propagation of the Gospel among our Mahometan and Gen-
too subjects in India'. Raikes further declared that it would be
found 'perhaps no less necessary to propagate the Gospel in our
own country', since one minister, whose parish bordered the Forest of Dean, frequently visited 'people in their last moments, who
(had) never heard of Jesus Christ, or been taught during their
lives to offer up a prayer to a Deity'. This clergyman maintained it
was deplorable that 'such unhappy wretches leave this world in a
state of brutal stupidity'.[16]

By the following September, however, at least one Sunday
school had been opened in the Forest of Dean, in the village of
Mitcheldean. Here a benefactor had sent money to one of the
trustees to provide 'a three-penny loaf to each of the poor children, who avail themselves of the institution for their instruction
on Sundays'. Raikes' correspondent added, 'It would have given
great delight to the donor to have seen how thankfully his present was received' and Raikes' comment was, 'Such little encouragements have a great effect in exciting among the children an
emulation to deserve the notice of their superiors, by a quiet and
orderly behaviour.'[17]

Raikes also mentioned in the same editorial that on the following Sunday, 2 October, 1785, an enquiry was to be held by the

promotors into the 'progress and beneficial effects' of Painswick Sunday School. On that day too a Revd Mr Fearon was to preach a charity sermon and the 'Musical Society' was to render anthems. Raikes made the success of this Sunday school the subject of a letter, which received wide publicity.

Besides helping to improve the behaviour of the neglected children Raikes expressed the hope that Sunday schools would be a means of protecting the children from bad associations and temptations which often led to criminal activities. The incidence of crime was increasing in Gloucestershire and Raikes made it known that those convicted were not mostly vagrants and wandering ne'er-do-wells, but were from the ignorant and wayward poor of the county. 'The number of commitments to the castle last week were not less than six,' reported Raikes in June, 1783. 'The prison is already so full, that all the gaoler's stock of fetters is occupied, and the smiths are hard at work in forging new ones. Could unhappy wretches see the misery that awaits them in a crowded gaol, they would surely relinquish the gratifications that reduce them to such a state of wretchedness. The people sent in are neither disbanded soldiers nor sailors, but chiefly inhabitants of the country (rural areas), frequenters of alehouses and skittle alleys.'[18]

Raikes, in common with leaders of contemporary society, saw drink as a vicious evil which led to moral disaster and crime and he believed instruction in Sunday schools to be the badly needed antidote. He constantly warned his readers of the dangers of visiting public houses: that drunkenness led to 'the destruction of health and comfort' and 'the subversion of order and good morals'.[19] He reminded farmers and 'unwary people' who had some distance to travel to their homes that, 'All who make too free with the glass, will certainly be watched and waylaid.'[20]

Raikes knew that money spent by indigent parents on drink not only wasted slender resources needed for feeding and clothing themselves and their children, but sometimes led to intoxication resulting in irresponsible, brutal behaviour. In reporting the following incident Raikes left his readers in no doubt of his own detestation of drunkenness. 'On Whit Monday Charles Jenkins, a shoemaker, of Nibley, near Sodbury, repairing, as usual with the common people in holiday time, to the ale-house, became extremely intoxicated, and went home about one in the morning;

where, finding his wife in bed with her four little ones, he took a board, which was fixed in the side of the bed to keep the children from falling out, and most barbarously murdered her, by beating her with the edge of the board till she expired. Some women, who lived near, awakened by the dreadful shrieks and groans of the wife, came and listened at the door, but were afraid to enter the house. They heard the unhappy creature, in most moving terms, imploring mercy; the poor little children too, with the most piercing cries and intreaties, were interceding for their mother, but the bloodthirsty villain, insensible to their tears, was not to be moved. The constable, who brought him to gaol, said the corpse was the most shocking mangled spectacle ever seen. – Whilst the irons were rivetting on his legs, the wretch trembled from head to foot.'[21] Jenkins was hanged the following July.

The corrupting influence of the company found in public houses was often blamed by those about to be executed. When four prisoners were executed in Gloucester in August, 1784, one of them, a James Bond, was reported to have 'made a pathetic speech to the crowd; assuring them, that the cause of their fatal end was loitering and sotting in ale houses'.[22] The following April, after eight men were hanged at the Gloucester County gallows for various offences, Raikes observed, 'The general plea used by these, as by all other criminals, was, that the profanation of the Lord's Day was the first step, and public houses the completion of their ruin.'[23]

Raikes not only advertised the work of the Sunday schools and their influence on children, but he also portrayed the causes and effects of crime. He linked godless upbringing with criminal end. He strove to engage the sympathy and support of the well-to-do amongst his readers for Sunday schools, by drawing attention to the deplorable situation and its roots, as well as offering by comparison the beneficial effects of Sunday schools on children's behaviour.

Raikes repeatedly publicised the misery and fatalities amongst those being punished for crime. He reported news of the life expectancy of prisoners sent from Gloucester gaol to serve sentences on the hulks. 'Of 21 convicts sent off from our castle to the Thames, in Dec., 1783, seven only are living.'[24] His reasons for this were several: to deter others from lawbreaking, and to help bring about prison reform, but chiefly to show the need of social, moral and religious discipline among the poor, and, of course, to underline the importance of establishment and support of Sunday schools.

Any misapprehension that the criminal classes were exclusively mature, hardened adults was dispelled by Raikes' coverage of the reports of a Parliamentary Committee in 1784 and by his stated belief that the numbers of criminals were increased annually by the corruption of young people. 'Nothing can more strongly evince the necessity of some general efforts to reclaim the rising generation of the lower class, than the report of the committee of the House of Commons investigating the subject of the prisons; from whose inquiries it appears, that one third of the criminals in the kingdom sentenced to transportation are under seventeen years of age.'[25]

It was against the ignorance, illiteracy and absence of moral instruction, all features abundantly exhibited by the criminal element of the time, that Raikes mounted his publicity campaign. For example, of the eight malefactors executed on 15 April, 1785, Raikes wrote in his paper they were '. . . all very ignorant and illiterate. Only one out of the eight had been taught to read, previous to their commitment to prison'.[26] James Hawkins was hanged for housebreaking in August the same year: 'Tho little more than 21 years of age he was a shocking instance of villainy which pervades the human heart, when the mind is destitute of every principle, and ignorance and vice are free from that restraint, which a knowledge of our duty is known to impose,' stated Raikes. 'He had never received the smallest instruction. He had never offered up a prayer to his Creator. He said he knew not how to pray. He was totally devoid of all sense of a future state.'[27]

In the April following Raikes made a similar observation. 'Of sixteen persons capitally convicted at our assizes, Ten are left for execution – It is a melancholy reflection that the enormities which prevail in this county, require such atonement to the offended laws. – Yet in the present state of ignorance, what can be expected of wretches who are on a level with the most unenlightened and savage nations. – It was recommended to some of the condemned to employ the few days they had to live, in repentance and prayer. – "Prayer," says one of them, "I cannot pray, – I never prayed – I never learned to pray – I would give the world I now could pray." One of them when sentence was passed, fell on his knees, and cried out, "My Lord, pray spare my life, . . . I am no more fit to die than you be;" – and when the keeper took him from the bar, he exclaimed, "If I am hanged, I shall go to Hell, cloaths and all!"'[28]

The danger of neglecting to give religious instruction to children was made evident by Raikes in publishing regularly reported confessions of criminals at the gallows. John Bliss, a native of Churchdown, near Gloucester, 'one of the most notorious villains our county has ever produced . . . made ample confessions of his crimes which,' declared Raikes, 'he ascribed to the shameful example and vile conduct of his father, who made the Sabbath a day of pastime and recreation for his children, treating every religious ordinance with contempt. This, he said, confirmed in his mind a degree of insensibility to every serious impression, and excited him to the commission of crimes which at length had brought him to this shameful exit.'[29] Griffiths (hanged on the same day as Bliss) had spurned the opportunity for instruction offered by a Sunday school founder. 'I wish,' Raikes reported Griffiths to have said, 'to leave this world; in which I should, perhaps, commit still greater crimes, and only increase my guilt. I lay the root of my sorrow to the contempt, with which I treated the friendship of the Rev. Mr Simpson of Macclesfield, who invited me with many others to partake of the instruction he provided to employ our time profitably on Sundays, but I preferred idling and loitering in the field, and now find too late the sad effects of my folly. May my sad fate teach others to make a better choice.'[30]

Those who suffered the death penalty were not dispatched quickly. Some minutes elapsed before they were strangled by the rope which was tightened by their body weight when the cart moved away and their distorted features changed colour in death. The grisly spectacle excited rather than disgusted those who attended the hangings. Crowds flocked to the scene to obtain a clear view of proceedings at the gallows. Raikes' detailed and vivid reports would prove disturbing to sensitive readers, as no doubt he intended that they should. The following account, which was recorded in the *Gloucester Journal* of 24 April, 1786, gives an idea of what spectators witnessed and of their numbers: 'Friday morning afforded a dismal spectacle. Nine criminals were carried in two carts to the place of execution. In the first went

Crew, Chapman in his shroud, Matthews, and Allaway; in the second, Whittick, Fry, Ward, Russ, and Davis. – The numbers which came from all parts of the country, for 20 miles round, to view this affecting sight, were supposed to amount to no less than ten thousand.

'At the place of execution the criminals behaved with becoming decency. Crew exhorted the beholders, with an audible voice, to shun the ways of sin, for there is no pleasure in them. – I speak, says he, from fatal experience; and you may be assured, that a man in my situation has no motive to deceive. Therefore, acquaint yourselves with God, and be at peace. Make the Sabbath a day of holiness unto the Lord, and then it will become to you a blessing. I know that the fear of God is in this world regarded as the effect of a cowardly or superstitious spirit; but when the aweful moment of death approaches; when, like me, you stand on the brink of eternity, then you will find that a daring temper will desert you, and fears and terrors will succeed. – Take warning then before it be too late.

'Matthews exhorted the people to be diligent in their business, and content with the earnings of their labour. – If you take home, said he, what you get, and share it with your families, you will find much greater enjoyment, than from spending your money in public houses; – frequenting those places on the Sabbath Day has been my ruin – Chapman joined in exhortations to the same effect; and added, Thieving is a poor business. I never gained much by it at the best; and now I pay my life for it.

'The carts were both set in motion at the same instant; and when the poor wretches fell, the whole crowd seemed with one consent to utter a groan of commiseration.

'An incident occurred which increased this aweful impression. Just as the malefactors were turned off, two strong flashes of lightening burst from a cloud, attended with thunder.'

Hanging, averred Raikes, was ineffective as a deterrent to crime. In August, 1785, he wrote, 'Though so many criminals have been hanged lately for horse stealing, yet even capital punishments seem to have no force in deterring offenders.'[31] Raikes hoped others would see, as clearly as he did himself, that the whole paraphernalia of the law, police, prisons, penal colonies, and gibbets, would never remove the gross, brutish ignorance of the uninstructed labouring people. As the child is the father of the man, only by teaching the children could the behaviour of the adults be changed. Authorities gradually concurred with Raikes' ideas. The magistrates themselves at the General Quarter Sessions of February, 1788, applauded the attempts in Sunday schools at the prevention of crime by instruction of the children. 'The benefit of Sunday Schools to the morals of the rising generation, is too evident, not to merit the recommendation of this bench, and the thanks of the community, to the gentlemen instrumental in promoting them.'[32]

Again and again Raikes addressed his readers on the importance of prison reform and the establishment of Sunday schools. Many clergymen, he reported, believed that children could by Sunday instruction be prevented from engaging in a life of crime. 'Whilst the public spirited exertions of the most distinguished characters in our country are meditating a reform of the police, by rendering our prisons, if possible, the very reverse of what they have hitherto been, seminaries of every species of villainy and profligacy;' wrote Raikes in his editorial of 24 May, 1784, ' – several of the clergy in the county are setting forward a mode of general instruction for the children of the lower class of people, by establishing schools for their reception upon Sundays; a day upon which they are given up to follow their wild and vicious inclinations free from restraint. The promoters of this design seem to concur in the idea, that prevention is better than punishment, and that any attempt to check the growth of vice at an early period, by an effort to introduce good habits of acting and thinking among the vulgar, is at least an experiment harmless and innocent, however fruitless it may prove in its effect.'

The frequently repeated argument was quickly extended nationwide by other editors using Raikes' articles and approaches in their newspapers, but the Church response came initially, as has been indicated already, from lowly, devout ministers and lay church members. High ecclesiastics were hesitant in embarking upon the new phenomenon of Sunday schools. When in May, 1784, Raikes printed a letter from a clergyman who had established a Sunday school the previous January, Raikes was careful to leave out positive means of identification. It was headed 'Extract of a letter from the Rev. Mr –,' and began, 'The plan of a Sunday School is much approved of here. Indeed, if every clergyman thought as I do, I am persuaded that no parish would long be without such seminary for the general reception of all children, who have no other means or leisure to acquire an idea of the relation in which every human stands with respect to his creator and his fellow creatures. Impressions made at this early period of life, are often found to have a very permanent and happy effect.' The clergyman then expressed his pleasure in the influence the Sunday school was having upon both the children and the community, and described how youngsters who had formerly spent Sundays 'in idleness and vice' were learning the principles of Christianity, and concluded by stating he was persuaded that the Sunday school would 'work a reformation of manners, and cause true religion to revive' in N . . . . . d.[33]

A breakthrough to recognition came in 1786 when that 'eminent divine', the Revd Dr Kay, Almoner to the Queen, during a visit to Nottingham gave a charge to 'the whole body of the Clergy in that county'. This was received with such satisfaction that many of them requested that the sermon should be sent to 'the printer of the Gloucester Journal'. On 6 February, 1786, Raikes devoted two columns to reproducing it although it contained nothing not already argued publicly by him. But to his message, summarised below, Kay lent the authority of his office. The 'late increase of capital crimes' came 'from the universal depravity of the people', and the measure which appeared to possess the 'invaluable antidote to the poisonous manners of this depraved age', was the establishment of Sunday schools. Not only would the children benefit, but members of their families would be affected, and the neighbourhood in which they lived. 'This object, my Reverend Brethren,' he concluded, 'I own to you, is nearest my heart in my present communication with you. It is a measure so unequivocal in the principles, so universal in its extent, so providentially pointed out to correct the degeneracy of the present age, and to prevent its evils from descending to future times, that you cannot employ your influence in more humanity to individuals, and more patriotism to your country, than by giving it every assistance and protection in your power.' Kay's charge proved compelling.

Episcopal support for Sunday schools stemmed from a change of mind by Beilby Porteous, Bishop of Chester. Initially disposed to approve and encourage Sunday schools he then had apprehensions about them, but finally decided that they had 'real value' if adopted in accordance with some qualifications and restrictions suggested by him. In a letter to his clergy, a verbatim copy of which Raikes printed in the *Gloucester Journal*, 15 May, 1786, Porteous admitted that the 'penal code (was) sufficiently sanguinary, and . . . executions sufficiently numerous, to strike terror (if that alone would do) into the populace' but that 'they (had) not hitherto produced any material alteration for the better'. He argued that 'laws without manners . . . avail nothing' and that 'manners (could) no otherwise be regulated than by a right education, by impressing on the minds of youth principles and habits of piety and virtue'; that while 'the expense of founding and supporting' Charity Schools necessarily prevented them 'from becoming universal', the financing of the Sunday schools, on the other hand, was 'so easy to be raised . . . the whole expence of instructing 20 children, including books, rewards, and every other charge, (would) not amount to £5 a year.' Sunday schools, he said, 'are most necessary and most useful in the great manufacturing towns, where there is the greatest number of children that want education, and who being in constant employment during the rest of the week, have scarcely any leisure allowed them for instruction but on the Lord's Day.'

In thus commending the establishment of Sunday schools Porteous defined clearly, as he saw it, their purpose. 'The very small degree of learning which is or can be given in these schools, though highly useful to their minds, does not either indispose or disqualify them from undertaking with their hands the most laborious employments in town and country. They are merely taught to read, and to make proper use of their Prayer Books, their Bibles, and a few pious tracts which inculcate the fear of God, and the love of man; which enjoin, under pain of eternal punishment, and with the promise of eternal rewards, the great duties of sobriety, industry, veracity, honesty, humility, patience, content, resignation to the will of God, and submission to the authority of their superiors . . . But this is not all. The greater part of the children educated in Sunday Schools are not merely taught to be diligent and laborious by words and precepts, but, what is far more useful and efficacious, they are actually trained up from their childhood in habits of industry. They consist, for the most part, of such as are employed in trades, manufactures, or husbandry work: to these they give up six days in the week, and on the remaining one (the Lord's Day) they are instructed in the rudiments of Christian faith and practice.'[34]

A copy of a second letter from the bishop to his clergy filled two columns of the next edition of the *Gloucester Journal*. In this Porteous observed that the Sunday schools, 'established near two years' in his Chester diocese, their 'good influence' was apparent in 'a visible alteration for the better' of the appearance and conduct of the children, and the 'sense of virtue and religion' which had 'manifestly communicated itself to the parents'. But in his reflections he analysed a problem which many zealous Sunday school organisers were ignoring – the needs of children who laboured six days out of seven. 'Though the great and principal design of the Lord's Day is to draw off our thoughts from worldly objects, to fix them on the concerns of eternity, and unite us in the acts of social worship to our Maker; yet it is also meant, both in its original institution, and its subsequent accommodation to the Christian system, to be a day of rest, and ease and comfort to all, but especially to the lower classes of the people, whose lot it commonly is to earn their daily bread by daily toil. To these, the Sunday is a most seasonable and salutary relief . . . But there is reason to fear that this will not be the case, if almost every hour of the Sunday is taken up either at Church or at School, and little or no interval allowed the Scholars for ease and inoffensive amusement. The business, and discipline, and confinement of a school, are things in some degree always unpleasant to young people, and if they are too rigorously enforced, with scarce any intermission, they will grow burdensome and painful; and these ideas being associated with those of going to church and worshipping God, will be apt to give the children a disgust for those duties, and even for the day itself on which they recur. And if this disgust grows up with, and gains strength with their years, it may tend to make them irreligious and profane.

'The utmost care therefore must be taken to guard against these fatal consequences. The scholars educated in the Sunday Schools must have sufficient time allowed them for cheerful conversation and free intercourse with each other, and, above all, for enjoying the fresh and wholesome air and sunshine, in the fields or gardens, with their relations or friends . . . I should think that four, or at the most five, hours in the school each Sunday would be confinement fully sufficient for children so circumstanced . . .

rather than intrench too much on the ease, and comfort, and cheerfulness of the day I would give up all learning that could be acquired by such means, and be content with the other great advantages of the institution. It is the discipline of the heart, more than the instruction of the head, for which Sunday Schools are chiefly valuable . . .

'Upon the same principle just mentioned, of preserving as much as possible the cheerful aspect of the Lord's Day, I should hope that no kind of severe correction would ever find its way into Sunday Schools. The infliction of any corporal punishment would probably render the day odious to the young sufferers, and give them unfavourable impressions of it, and everything belonging to it, as long as they lived. These institutions must be founded on a system not of severity, but of kindness, of persuasion, of encouragement, of reward.' Raikes, himself, could have learned a great deal from Bishop Porteous, but perhaps the reverse might also have been true.

In whatever regard Raikes held the Bishop of Chester's 'qualifications and restrictions', he must have felt satisfaction in the realisation that other bishops would follow Beilby Porteous' lead in supporting the establishment of Sunday schools. Only two months later Raikes must have been especially heartened when he learned that on his first triennial visitation to the Cathedral, Samuel Halifax, Bishop of Gloucester, in his address to the clergy, was pleased 'to make favourable mention of Sunday Schools, which he doubted not, with proper management, and under the inspection of the parochial clergy, might be productive of great good, among the children of the poor, throughout his diocese.'[35] It was absolutely certain now that the Sunday school would become a national institution.

The publicity given to Sunday schools by Raikes was such that he personally became identified with them. He was regarded as one of their staunchest supporters – their champion. When, therefore, 'the produce' of a play performed in Gloucester for the benefit of Sunday schools was not 'publicly acknowledged' in the *Gloucester Journal,* a letter of protest was sent to the editor. Raikes explained that it was no oversight and that 'he had no concern in the scheme and the persons engaged in the performance (had) never communicated to him any particulars on the subject'.[36]

Raikes corresponded with a number of people interested in

Sunday schools and some of those letters were published in newspapers and magazines. Richard Townley, to whose inquiry Raikes replied on 25 November, 1783, giving an account of the Sunday schools in Gloucester, asked for and obtained Raikes' permission to publish his letter 'in such country journals or newspapers as (he, Townley) thought proper'.[37] Then on 26 December, 1783, Townley wrote to two northern newspapers and Raikes' letter appeared in the *Manchester Mercury* on 6 January, 1784 and the *Leeds Intelligencer* on 13 January, 1784.

Raikes' letter had strongly influenced Townley. He felt that when read the letter would 'speak for itself, and in a language too not only convincing, but highly pleasing to every person possessed of true benevolence, and hearty good-will for our fellow creatures, especially those who stand so much in need thereof, as Children of poor Labourers and Manufacturers, many thousands of whom now are, and forever must be, abandoned to the most gross, as well as pitiable ignorance, without some charitable aid'.[38] His own well reasoned, if lengthy, comments on the letter suggesting that there 'should be a strong inducement to adopt Mr Raikes' humane and excellent plan, or one nearly similar to it' in the 'Northern parts' of the country, were also published in the *Leeds Intelligencer*.[39] Townley, in a series of articles to the press, called upon the magistracy to approve Raikes' ideas and to recommend that overseers of the poor and churchwardens should establish Sunday schools. Financial aid for the schools, he suggested, might come from fines imposed on those using obscene language, etc, as well as from collections at church.[40]

Raikes' letter was also printed in the *Gentleman's Magazine*, June, 1784, having been sent to its editor by 'A FRIEND TO VIRTUE' from Sheffield, with the recommendation that 'The importance of the subject, and the benevolent manner in which it is expressed, justly entitle it to the attentive regard of every virtuous man.' The editor of the *Gentleman's Magazine*, a friend of Raikes, three-starred his remark after the subscription of the letter. 'It is with pleasure we give place to this benevolent plan; which promises fair to transmit the name of Mr Raikes to later posterity.'

An upsurge of the Sunday School Movement in the northern counties came shortly after the publication of Raikes' letter. As Raikes reported, by May 1784, Leeds Sunday schools had 2,000 scholars. An announcement of the expansion of Sunday schools in Manchester appeared in the *Manchester Mercury* on 10 August, 1784, and a week later its readers were informed of a gift of spelling books from Raikes. In the same month it was reported that Sunday schools had been opened in Rochdale and Bury. Northern newspapers, in the years that followed, frequently included accounts of the setting up of new Sunday schools and their encouraging, even astounding, achievements.[41]

The initial stimulus and helpful correspondence provided by Raikes resulted in a new, important development in the expansion of the Sunday School Movement – the Sunday School Society. William Fox, a native of the Gloucestershire village of Clapton, near Bourton-on-the-Water, of humble beginnings, after varied fortunes in business, and the recovery from a near fatal fever, became prosperous in the wholesale business in London. Friendship with his minister, the Revd Mr Booth, resulted in his becoming a deacon of Prescott Street Church, London, and devoting some of his affluence to helping those in need and, having his attention drawn to Raikes' letter in the papers, wrote thus to Raikes on 15 June, 1785.

'Sir, The liberality and goodness of heart manifested in your benevolent plan of Sunday Schools, will, I trust, render unnecessary any apology, though from a stranger, when it is considered, his only view in writing is, that he may be enabled to copy after so worthy an example.' Fox then explained that before Raikes' 'excellent letter appeared in the papers' he had himself set up a school 'for the indigent and ignorant poor' at Clapton, but that it had involved 'far greater expence, and, perhaps, less utility' than the Sunday schools of Raikes, whom he asked, therefore, for further details of his 'plan'. Fox also expressed doubts of the possibility of teaching children to read who only attended school 'one day in seven'. The importance of receiving a reply from Raikes was, he said, 'because a society is forming in town, to which I belong, for carrying a plan of this sort into general use', and he added, 'The design, I dare say, will appear to you laudable, but at the same time difficult: its success depends on the concurrence and aid of well disposed christians throughout the kingdom.' Fox obviously required sound answers to questions likely to be raised.

Raikes replied on 20 June, 1785, almost by return, yet apologising for being out of town, otherwise he said, he would have replied sooner. He said that Fox's apology for his letter was utterly unnecessary and that he was 'full of admiration at the great, the noble design' of the society Fox spoke of forming. He informed Fox that he had written a letter to Jonas Hanway (the London philanthropist and champion of poor children), upon the subject of Sunday schools, only the week before, and suggested, 'If you ask him for a sight of it, I dare say he will send it to you'. Raikes also gave some reassuring answers to Fox concerning the teaching of reading, quoting two people who had called to see him. One, a clergyman, said Raikes, had that very afternoon expressed surprise at the progress made in the Sunday school at Painswick, and had declared, 'Many boys now can read, who certainly have no other opportunity than what they derive from their Sunday instruction.' Raikes' other visitor reported on the Sunday school in Mitcheldean, in the Forest of Dean, 'among the children of the colliers, a most savage race' that it now had 'many children who, three months ago, knew not a letter from a cart wheel, who can now repeat hymns in a manner that would astonish you'. Raikes ended his letter with a promise of help. 'When you have seen my letter to Mr Hanway, you will be able to judge whether farther use can be made of the little experience I have had, in this attempt at civilisation. I can only say, show wherein I may be useful, and command without reserve.'

The society to which Fox belonged approved Fox's suggestions and it was agreed that a letter should be sent to various individuals with a view to arranging 'a more general meeting'.[42] The letter bearing Fox's signature outlined the steps taken and those proposed.

'Sir, Encouraged by the promising success of the Sunday Schools established in some towns and villages of this kingdom, several gentlemen met on Tuesday evening, the 16th instant, at the King's Head Tavern, in the Poultry, to consider of the utility of forming "A Society for the Establishment and Support of Sunday Schools, throughout the Kingdom of Great Britain."

'At this meeting it was agreed to form such a society; and a Committee of fourteen gentlemen was chosen to draw up a code of laws for the government of the said Society, and a set of proper rules for the regulation of the Schools.

'The Committee having met, and drawn up a plan of the intended Society, and the laws and rules necessary for it and the Schools, they propose to submit their plan to the consideration of all such gentlemen as shall attend a public meeting, to be holden on Tuesday next, the 30th instant, at the Paul's Head Tavern, Cateaton-Street, at four o'clock in the afternoon.

'To prevent vice – to encourage industry and virtue – to dispel the darkness of ignorance – to diffuse the light of knowledge – to bring men cheerfully to submit to their stations – to obey the laws of God and their country – to make that useful part of the community, the country poor, happy – to lead them in the pleasant paths of religion here – and to endeavour to prepare them for a glorious eternity, are the objects proposed by the prompters of this Institution.

'To effect these great, these noble ends, they hope to form a Society, which will be enabled to establish Sunday Schools, upon a plan so extensive as to reach the remotest parts of this island; and they flatter themselves they shall receive support, assistance, and patronage of persons of every rank and description.'[43]

Raikes was sent a copy of Fox's circularised letter by his brother Thomas; he wrote again to Fox regretting that he, personally, was unable to attend the meeting on the 30 August, 1785, but that he thought 'a sketch' he had made of 'the pleasing scene' on the first Sunday schools anniversary at Mitcheldean at which he had been present might prove interesting and useful if 'laid before the gentlemen who attend your summons to the Paul's Head Tavern'. Two gentlemen of property, Maynard Colchester and William Lane, had the previous Christmas 'established two schools', said Raikes, 'and admitted about fifty or sixty of both sexes; some of them the most ignorant, uncivilised beings in the country'. But the progress that had been made here, wrote Raikes, 'tends to prove the practicability of doing good to our fellow creatures . . . The children, though many of them in apparel very ragged, were extremely clean. They walked in great order, two and two, to the church, where they were placed in a gallery, exposed to the view of the whole congregation: and their behaviour, during the service, was perfectly silent and becoming.'[44]

Fox was delighted to receive Raikes' letter of 29 August, 1785, and he acted upon Raikes' suggestion to approach Hanway, and also invited Raikes' brother, Thomas, to join the committee. The help and encouragement given to Fox by Raikes in founding the Sunday School Society can perhaps be best inferred from Fox's letter to Raikes of 2 September, 1785. 'Presuming upon the

friendship with which you honoured me, and particularly
encouraged by your last favour, I took the liberty of waiting on
your brother, the Bank Director, to request his acceptance of the
Chair, well knowing how much depended upon such a choice.
Both your brothers received me with the greatest politeness and
cordiality; promised the design countenance and support; but
declined the Chair, as the Bank Director was just going out of
town. They then advised me to go to Mr Thornton, another Bank
Director; and your elder brother accompanied me to him. He also
made the same kind of offer of support &c. which your brother
had done, but was unfortunately going out of town likewise, and
advised me to apply to Mr Hanway, who took the Chair.'

Raikes and Fox continued their correspondence and certainly
made each other's acquaintance at the Painswick Sunday School
Anniversary, if not before. Probably at Fox's request (for Fox was
present and could have given the members of the committee his
own account) Raikes wrote a letter on 7 October, 1786, to the
Committee of the Sunday School Society describing the proceedings. Raikes' letter is included here, almost in its entirety, because
in it he depicted the beneficial influence of Sunday schools upon
the whole community and attributed 'liberality' and 'benevolence'
to those engaged in the work and because his letter received
nationwide publicity appearing both in the *Universal Magazine*[45]
and the *New Lady's Magazine* for February, 1787.

'The parish of Painswick exhibited on Sunday, the 24 (September, 1786), a specimen of the reform which the establishment
of Sunday Schools is likely to introduce. An annual feast has for
time immemorial been held on that day; a festival that would
have disgraced the most heathenish nations. Drunkenness, and
every species of clamour, riot, and disorder, formerly filled the
town upon this occasion.

'Mr Webb, a gentleman who has exerted the utmost assiduity
in the conduct of the Sunday Schools in Painswick, was lamenting to me the sad effects that might be naturally expected to arise
from this feast. It occurred to us that an attempt to divert the
attention of the vulgar from their former brutal prostitution of
Our Lord's-day, by exhibiting to their view a striking picture of
the superior enjoyment to be derived from quietness, good order,
and the exercise of that benevolence which Christianity peculiarly
recommends, was an experiment worth hazarding. We thought it

could do no mischief – it would not increase the evil. It was immediately determined to invite the gentlemen and people of the adjacent parishes to view the children of the Sunday Schools, to mark their improvement in cleanliness and behaviour, and to observe the practicability of reducing to a quiet, peacable demeanour, the most neglected part of the community, those who form the great bulk of the people.

'In the parish of Painswick are several gentlemen who have a taste for music; they immediately offered to give every assistance in the church service; and my benevolent friend, the Rev. Dr. Glasse, complied with our entreaty to favour us with a sermon . . .'

Raikes then appears to finish his letter by quoting from the report of a Mr Boddington of Cheltenham who had been invited to inspect the school. 'On the Sunday afternoon the town was filled with the usual crowds who attend the feast; but, instead of repairing to the ale-houses as heretofore, they all hastened to the church, which was filled in such a manner as I never remember to have seen in any church in this country before. The galleries, the aisles, were thronged like a playhouse. Drawn up in a rank around the church-yard, appeared the children belonging to the different schools, to the number of 331.

'The gentlemen walked round to view them; it was a sight interesting and truly affecting: young people, lately more neg-lected than the cattle in the field, ignorant, profane, filthy, clamorous, impatient of every restraint, were here seen cleanly, quiet, observant of order, submissive, courteous in behaviour, and in conversation free from that vileness which marks our wretched vulgar.

'The inhabitants of the town bear testimony to this change in their manners. The appearance of decency might be assumed for a day; but the people among whom they live are ready to declare that this is a character fairly stated.

'After the public service a collection for the benefit of the institution was made at the doors of the church. When I consi-dered that the bulk of the congregation were persons of middling rank, husbandmen, and other inhabitants of adjacent villages, I concluded that the collection, if it amounted to £24 or £25 might be deemed a good one. My astonishment was great, indeed, when I found the sum was not less than £57. This may be accounted for from the security which the establishment of Sunday Schools has given to the property of every individual in the neighbourhood. The farmers, etc., declare that they and their families can now leave their houses, gardens, etc., and frequent the public worship without danger of depredation. Formerly, they were under the necessity of leaving their servants or staying at home themselves as a guard; and this was insufficient; the most vigilant were sometimes plundered. It is not then to be wondered at, that a spirit of liberality was excited on this occasion . . .

'When the matter of the collection was settled, we went to the Schools, to hear what progress was made in reading, etc.

'The emulation to shew their acquirements was so very general, that it would have taken up a day to have gratified all the children.

'In the meantime, the town was remarkably free from those pastimes which used to disgrace it. Wrestling, quarrelling, fighting, were totally banished. All was peace and tranquility . . .

'I forgot to mention that Mr Fox, one of the worthy members of your Committee, was present with us at Painswick.

'The Sunday Schools were first established at Painswick in the summer of the year 1784. The children had been bred up in total ignorance. Of the number that attend the Schools, 230 can read in the Bible of Testament, 80 can read in the Sunday Scholars' Companion, and about 21 are in the alphabet. These children have no teaching but on the Sunday; what they learn at the leisure hours in the week is the effect of their own desire to improve. Many have their books at their looms, to seize any vacant minute, when their work is retarded by the breaking of threads.

'To relieve the parish from the burthen of cloathing (sic) these poor creatures, Mr Webb proposed that such children, as by an increase of industry would bring a penny every Sunday towards their cloathing, should be assisted by having that penny doubled. This has had an admirable effect; the children now regularly bring their pence every Sunday; many of them have been cloathed, and the good consequences of laying up a little are powerfully enforced.

'It is pretty evident that, were every parish in this kingdom blessed with a man or two of Mr Webb's active turn and benevolent mind, the lower class of people, in a few years, would exhibit a material change of character, and justify that superior policy which tends to prevent crimes, rather than to punish them. The liberality with which the members of your Society have stood forth, in this attempt to introduce a degree of civilisation and good order among the lower ranks, entitles them to the thanks of the community and particularly of an individual who will ever be proud to subscribe himself.'

After attending the Colchester Sunday School Anniversary Fox sent an account to Raikes, and in his reply Raikes requested his friend to send him a copy of the June, 1787 edition of the *World*, a paper in which the account had been published. Raikes also informed Fox of a remark made to his brother Thomas, by Adam Smith, the renowned economist and author of *The Wealth of Nations*. In this work Adam Smith had stressed the importance of instructing 'the inferior ranks of people'. 'The more they are instructed the less liable they are to the delusions of enthusiasm and superstition, which among ignorant nations, frequently occasion dreadful disorders. An instructed and intelligent people, besides, are always more decent and orderly than an ignorant and stupid one. They feel themselves, each individually, more respectable and more likely to obtain the respect of their lawful superiors, and they are therefore more disposed to respect those superiors.'[46] Thomas Raikes found occasion when the thinker and scholar was visiting London to talk to him about Sunday schools, and the elderly Smith's enthusiastic response, 'No plan has promised to effect a change of manners with equal ease and simplicity since the days of the Apostles,'[47] Thomas must have communicated to his brother Robert in Gloucester. Anyway, although Thomas Raikes probably related Adam Smith's words to Fox himself, Robert made sure that the Founder of the Sunday School Society knew what the great thinker had said. Such a statement by Adam Smith merited publicity. Raikes also ensured that the work of the Sunday School Society received publicity by regularly reporting in his newspaper the number of Sunday schools founded and children attending them.

It was perhaps not too surprising to Raikes to learn that on 11 July, 1787 the general meeting of the Sunday School Society had resolved unanimously 'that in consideration of the zeal and merits of Robert Raikes Esq., of Gloucester, who may be considered the original founder, as well as a liberal promoter, of Sunday Schools, he be admitted an honorary member of this society'. This resolution must have afforded Raikes immense pleasure as did knowledge of the progress made by the Society in promoting Sunday schools. By January, 1791, it had established or assisted in establishing 746 schools, with an attendance of 49,379 scholars.[48]

More of Raikes' letters were published in the national press. John Nichols, the well-known printer and publisher of the *Gentleman's Magazine*, who had already published Raikes' first letter to Richard Townley, decided after receiving a personal letter from Raikes in 1787 that the content would interest his readers. He therefore printed it in the *Gentleman's Magazine*, adding the placatory comment, 'Mr Raikes' own good heart will pardon our thus divulging it'. Raikes, indeed, would have welcomed publicising the almost unbelievable speed with which the Sunday School Movement was developing. 'It is incredible with what rapidity this "grain of mustard seed" has extended its branches over the nation. The third of this month (November) completes four years since I first mentioned the expediency of Sunday Schools in *The Gloucester Journal*, and by the best information I am assured that the number of poor children who were heretofore as neglected as the wild ass's colt, but who are now taken into these seminaries of instruction amounts to 250,000. In the town of Manchester alone the schools contain 5,000. It would delight you to observe the cheerfulness with which the children attend on the Sunday. A Woman told me last Sunday that her boy enquires of her every night before he goes to bed whether he has done anything that will furnish a complaint against him on Sunday. You, see, sir, to what care and vigilance this may lead.'[49] Prior to this the *Arminian Magazine*, edited by John Wesley, had carried a letter from Raikes dated 5 June, 1785[50] in which he described the founding of the four Sunday schools in Gloucester supported by the Revd Thomas Stock and himself. Wesley too fully approved of Sunday schools describing them as 'one of the noblest specimens of charity which have been set on foot in England since the time of William the Conqueror.'[51] Furthermore in a letter dated 18 July, 1784, written after preaching at Bingley in Yorkshire, Wesley gave this description. 'Before service I stepped into the Sunday School . . . So many children in one parish restrained from open sin, and taught a little good manners at least, as well as to read the Bible.'[52]

The extensive publicity provided by Raikes through his personal associations, through his newspaper, and through his letters in which he had described Sunday schools brought him unsought fame. In spite of no reference whatsoever being made in the *Gloucester Journal* to his involvement in the work of Sunday schools, a public image of Raikes was created as the 'Founder of Sunday Schools', and through that 'image', the magnificence of which he genuinely seemed to enjoy, the name Robert Raikes of Gloucester became synonymous with that of the Sunday School Movement.

Raikes gained unexpected fame for himself and the Sunday schools when he reported in the *Gloucester Journal* the sad case of Anne Yearsley, a milkwoman of Bristol, and subsequently promoted the publishing of her poems. 'The poor woman, surrounded by four children and an aged mother, was found by a benevolent gentleman in a little cottage near Clifton . . . perishing from want, having been three days without sustenance.'[53] When some verses written by Mrs Yearsley were seen she was declared to be a 'poetical prodigy' and a volume of 'Poems on Several Occasions' by the 'Bristol poetess' was published in 1785. One of the poems entitled *On Promoting Sunday Schools* was an 178 line effusion eulogising the Sunday schools and Raikes. Thanks to the patronage of Hannah More, then 'at the height of her literary and social fame in London',[54] the list of subscribers was incredible. There were some 1,002 among whom were to be found such famous names as Horace Walpole, Sir Joshua Reynolds, William Blake, Dr and Miss Burney, as well as numerous Dukes, Duchesses, Countesses and Bishops. Presumably most of them read the poem and thus became acquainted with the benevolent efforts of Raikes.

The sermon entitled *The Piety, Wisdom, and Policy of Promoting Sunday Schools* preached by Samuel Glasse, DD, FRS, Rector of Wanstead, Essex, and Chaplain Ordinary to his Majesty, at Painswick Church on the occasion of the Sunday School Anniversary was dedicated 'To Mr Robert Raikes of the City of Gloucester, An Instructor of the Ignorant and a Father to the Poor, To whose piety and zeal, in the first institution and the subsequent encouragement of Sunday Schools, every friend of religion is indebted.' The sermon, which was published in London and sold widely, contained references to the Bishop of Chester's letter, and a sermon by the Dean of Canterbury. In it too were many statements about approval and support which Sunday schools were receiving. 'Both the Archbishops, and many other Prelates, particularly the Lord Bishop of the Diocese in which this sermon was preached,' wrote Glasse, 'have, I understand, been pleased warmly to recommend them (Sunday schools) in their charges at their respective visitations.'[55] Later in his sermon he spoke of the contribution being made by the owner of Tortworth Castle, Gloucestershire. 'The wisdom of inuring the Poor to habits of good management and frugality, to the want of which is owing a great part of their distresses, hath so forcibly struck the mind of that worthy Nobleman, Lord Ducie, that, throughout a large district, he has offered to double every sum saved by poor children, to procure them cloathes.'[56] Such savings, like those of the children at Painswick Sunday school, were associated with the children's Sunday school and church attendance. The appendix to the sermon included an interesting pronouncement of an eminent Roman Catholic Priest in Ireland which began, 'The plan of Sunday schools meets with my warmest approbation . . . To the eternal honour of the worthy Associates in this good work, the plan is making rapid progress towards rescuing the lower classes from ignorance, and its concomitant licentiousness.'[57]

Further references to Raikes as the 'Father of the Poor' and 'a friend of mankind' were made by the Revd Samuel Glasse.[58] Besides the account of Raikes' philanthropic work in Gloucester gaol, already quoted, Glasse described Raikes' labours with children on Sundays and concluded his narrative thus: 'It is now a period of four years since this institution was first set on foot; and this grain of mustard-seed is now grown to such an incredible extent, that, under its shadow, not fewer than 250,000 of our poor fellow-Christians are sheltered and protected. Fronɩ this spark, excited by the zeal, and supported by the indefatigable attention, of a worthy individual, such a flame of piety and charity has been kindled, as diffuses its brightness through our own and a neighbouring kingdom, and is even about to extend itself to our settlements in distant countries, comprehending all descriptions of the poor, and affording a most delightful prospect, to every serious mind, of a national reformation of manners among the lower orders of the people.'

The European Magazine and London Review for November, 1788 carried 'An Account of Mr Robert Raikes, Founder of the Sunday

Schools' together with a portrait of him. The opening paragraph made it clear that anyone seeking to be virtuous needed simply to emulate Raikes.

'Neither high birth nor literary distinction claims our present attention,' stated the writer. 'The splendour of the one, and the brilliancy of the other, we think of inferior consideration when compared with the merits of persons by whose means knowledge is diffused, order and subordination preserved, infant virtue cherished, and religious principles inculcated and impressed. We therefore esteem it a duty to bring to the notice of the world a gentleman to whose exertions the present times are indebted for a plan, the operation of which, if diligently attended to, will be felt by the latest posterity; a plan simple in itself, easy to be carried into execution, favourable to the happiness of individuals, and in a high degree beneficial to the community at large. To services like these how insignificant the common objects of attention in mankind appear in the comparison.'

Jonas Hanway, nationally famous for the invention of the umbrella and for bringing public notice to the sufferings of climbing boys in his *Sentimental History of Chimney Sweeps* published in 1785, also paid tribute to Raikes. Accompanying his work *A Comprehensive View of Sunday Schools* published in London in 1786 he presented a document entitled *An Advertisement to the Most Intelligent Friends of the Institution of Sunday Schools* and in this Hanway wrote, 'The institution of the Sunday School is the production of the humanity and pious hopes of Mr. Raikes, a gentleman of Gloucester.'

Sarah Trimmer, a writer of books for children, founded Sunday schools in Brentford in 1786, and published her work, *The Economy of Charity* the same year. Dedicated to Queen Charlotte, Mrs Trimmer's publication, besides dealing at some length with the promotion and management of Sunday schools, was devoted particularly to persuading young 'well-to-do' ladies to assist in Sunday school teaching. Mrs Trimmer emphasised the point which Raikes had declared to be of paramount importance, *videlicet*, that the success of Sunday schools depended upon the involvement of people whose level of education was superior to that of the paid teachers and the children. In her work Mrs Trimmer mentioned the sermons of the Revd Samuel Glasse, the Revd Mr Ellis of Stroud, and the Revd John Bennet of Manchester, and

the Bishop of Chester's letter. Her praise of Raikes himself would
have helped to increase the regard in which he was held by many
of her aristocratic friends: 'Mr Raikes of Gloucester (whose name
every Christian must venerate) has, by his excellent scheme of
Sunday-schools drawn attention of the benevolent towards the
rising generation of the parish poor, who are already become
objects of general regard.'[59] The Queen, when she wished to set
up Sunday schools in Windsor, invited Mrs Trimmer on 19
November, 1786, to an interview, which lasted for two hours.

The culmination of Raikes' publicity campaign, personally
waged on behalf of the Sunday School Movement, came on 17
June, 1787. The newspapers carried the story. 'Mr Raikes, printer
of Gloucester, having received a card from Miss Planta, of her
Majesty's household at Windsor, attended there on Sunday 17
instant; and had the honour of being personally noticed by the
King and Queen, *"as the original institutor of Sunday Schools."* Their
Majesties expressed much pleasure at seeing him, and their royal
approbation of the zeal he had manifested in instituting this very
excellent mode of instructing the poor.'[60] Raikes was delighted by
the Queen's interest and later in a letter to the Revd Bowen
Thickens of Ross, he described the audience: 'The Queen sent for
me the other day to give Her Majesty an account of the effects
observable on the manners of the poor, and Her Majesty graciously said that she envied those who had the power of doing
good by thus personally promoting the welfare of society in giving instruction and morality to the general mass of the common
people, a pleasure from which by her position she was debarred.'[61] Raikes then, in wishful reflection, continued, 'Were this
known to the ladies of the British nation, it would serve to ani-
mate them with zeal and follow in the example which the Queen
is so desirous to set before them.'[62] Raikes knew that ladies of
fashion at Windsor taught poor children on Sundays, but any
hope he may have entertained of their example being followed
nationally would have been a forlorn one.

The publicity of the work of Sunday schools had succeeded
beyond Raikes' wildest expectations. His message had reached
members of all classes and sections of society: very poor labourers, farmers, and traders, entrepreneurs and bankers, writers and
poets, the Churches, Anglican, Methodist, Roman Catholic and
Quaker, the lesser clergy, bishops, even primates, Members of

both Houses of Parliament and the Sovereign. After Raikes' admission into the orbit of the royal sun respectability illumined those engaged in the work of Sunday schools. Raikes' mission had the approval of the lowest and the loftiest.

Raikes had tried to inform poor parents of their responsibilities and the benefits their children might derive from attendance at Sunday school, and he had encouraged those clergy undertaking the responsibility for the instruction of the children of the poor. He had repeatedly emphasised the importance of those who had themselves received an education accepting a role of leadership in Sunday schools. By his own example and through his personal correspondence he had inspired others. His proprietorship of the *Gloucester Journal* and his expertise as a journalist and editor ideally matched his own motivation. In the words of his co-worker and friend, the Revd Thomas Stock, 'The progress of this institution (the Sunday school) through the kingdom is justly to be attributed to the constant representations which Mr Raikes made in his own paper of the benefits which he perceived would probably arise from it.'[63] The public image of Raikes stirred the nation's moral conscience.

NOTES

[1] *The Sunday School Teachers' Magazine* (1830) p 683
[2] *Gloucester Journal* 3 April, 1786
[3] Joseph Stratford, *Robert Raikes and Others: The Founders of Sunday Schools* (1880) p 67
[4] J. H. Harris (editor), *Robert Raikes: The Man and his Work* p 145
[5] Ibid pp 146
[6] *Gloucester Journal* 25 October, 1784
[7] Ibid 16 February, 1784
[8] Ibid 8 November, 1784
[9] Ibid 29 March, 1784
[10] Ibid 16 February, 1784
[11] Ibid 8 November, 1784
[12] Ibid 15 November, 1784
[13] Ibid 20 December, 1784
[14] Ibid 3 January, 1785
[15] Ibid 6 March, 1786
[16] Ibid 4 April, 1785
[17] Ibid 25 September, 1785
[18] Ibid 9 June, 1783
[19] Ibid 27 February, 1786
[20] Ibid 29 November, 1784

[21] Ibid 23 May, 1785
[22] Ibid 16 August, 1784
[23] Ibid 18 April, 1785
[24] Ibid 3 January, 1785
[25] Ibid 22 March, 1784
[26] Ibid 18 April, 1785
[27] Ibid 8 August, 1785
[28] Ibid 3 April, 1786
[29] Ibid 18 April, 1785
[30] Ibid
[31] Ibid 22 August, 1785
[32] Ibid 4 February, 1788
[33] Ibid 24 May, 1784
[34] Ibid 15 May, 1786
[35] Ibid 3 July, 1786
[36] Ibid 2 May, 1785
[37] *Leeds Intelligencer* 13 January, 1784
[38] Ibid
[39] Ibid
[40] A. P. Wadsworth, *The First Manchester Sunday Schools: Bulletin of the John Rylands Library* No 33 (1951) p 304
[41] Ibid
[42] W. F. Lloyd, *Sketch of the Life of Robert Raikes* (1826) p 30
[43] William Fox, *Letter* 26 August, 1785
[44] Raikes, *Letter* 29 August, 1785
[45] *Universal Magazine* Vol LXXIX pp 361, 362
[46] Adam Smith, *The Wealth of Nations* (Everyman 1938) Vol II p 269
[47] F. W. Hirst, *Adam Smith* (1904) p 228
[48] Report of the General Meeting of the Sunday School Society 12 January, 1791 quoted in *The Sunday School Teachers' Magazine* (1830)
[49] Alfred Gregory, *Robert Raikes: Journalist and Philanthropist* (1880) p 82
[50] Ibid p 51
[51] Ibid p 76
[52] P. M. Eastman (editor), *Robert Raikes and Northamptonshire Sunday Schools* (1880) p 13
[53] *Gloucester Journal* 20 December, 1784
[54] M. G. Jones, *Hannah More* (1952) p 73
[55] Samuel Glasse, *The Piety, Wisdom, and Policy of Promoting Sunday Schools* p 14
[56] Ibid p 19
[57] Ibid p 29
[58] 'A Short Sketch of the Life of Robert Raikes', *Gentleman's Magazine* 1788 Vol LVIII (i) pp 11–15
[59] Sarah Trimmer, *The Economy of Charity* (1787) p 14
[60] *Leeds Intelligencer* 3 July, 1787
[61] Harris, op cit p 128
[62] Ibid
[63] Thomas Stock, *Letter* 2 February, 1788

Chapter 6
PIONEER OF POPULAR EDUCATION

Thanks in no small measure to Raikes and those of similar pioneering spirit the nation learned of the power of education. In increasing numbers people of all ranks and stations in society saw that it was in their own interests to have the poor instructed. After the publicity given to Sunday schools the great mass of the nation's children were viewed with a new sense of understanding. The common people themselves, parents and children, began to realise that schooling could effect remarkable changes advantageous to them. In communities throughout the kingdom attitudes of indifference changed to those of concern and caring. The tremendous significance of the Sunday School Movement, begun by Raikes, has never been adequately appraised. When full consideration is given to the changes in educational outlook following Raikes' publicity campaign and the establishment of Sunday schools throughout the country, it is difficult to conclude other than that Raikes was an outstanding pioneer of popular education.

Religious teaching was given by thousands to hundreds of thousands. Clergymen of all denominations became imbued with an increased sense of the importance of their calling. Sermons, in abundance, were preached and printed to justify the establishment of Sunday schools and the religious instruction of the children of the common people. A sermon preached by John Liddon on 30 September, 1792, and later published for the benefit of the Sunday schools at Hemel Hempstead, Hertfordshire, was entitled 'The general religious Instruction of the Poor, the surest Means of promoting universal Happiness'. Clergy and laymen maintained, like the writer of a pamphlet published on behalf of a Sunday school in Sunderland in 1790, that 'religious instruction is the great end serious people ought to propose in Sunday schools'.[1]

The importance to Raikes of a Christian outlook and of religious teaching in Sunday schools is made clear in the second sentence of his letter to a Mrs Harris of Chelsea, who was seeking information about his Sunday schools. 'I am rejoiced,' he wrote, 'to find that the people of your neighbourhood are thus ready to listen to that strong and pathetic injunction given by our Saviour a little before his ascension – "Feed my lambs".'[2] The food to which Christ referred was, of course, for spiritual as well as physical needs. An example of the spiritual comfort brought to a dying child by the religious teaching he had received in Sunday school was described by Raikes in November, 1784. 'Last week a poor boy, who attended one of the Sunday Schools of this city, died of a fever – The people, who were about him the last day or two of his illness, say, that as long as he was able to speak, he was continually repeating the prayers and hymns which he had learned at the school, and from which the child seemed to draw the highest comfort and satisfaction in his last moments.'[3]

Raikes was a leader among pioneers of social and moral education. He held strong views on cleanliness: cleanliness came next to godliness. At least the importance of a cleanly appearance was impressed upon the children. Whatever the state of their clothes, he insisted that Sunday school children should come with 'clean hands, clean face and hair combed'. John Howard was the authority whom Raikes quoted. This distinguished prison visitor, when asked how he avoided infection, replied that he trusted 'under God, to extreme cleanliness alone'. Then, in view of Howard's assertion, Raikes wrote, 'This is an additional recommendation to the comfort of that most valuable quality; a comfort the meanest might enjoy, if laziness and indolence did not obstruct them in the necessary exertion – Much of the fickleness with which the common people are afflicted, might be prevented, were due attention paid to cleanliness.'[4]

Raikes' great hope and endeavour was for a reformation of society. Unfortunately, we are not privileged to know the depth of his thinking: the kind of reformation appears to have been an open question to him. Raikes' letters and articles may seem vague, but they were in fact skilfully written and stimulating, without giving more than a brief hint at the possibilities. Those who were activated by Raikes' message pursued their own ideas, some of which were highly imaginative.

To effect changes in the social and ethical behaviour of the common people constituted a major consideration for Raikes. In reply to an inquiry from Bradford in May, 1784 Raikes gave what he described as a 'striking example' of the success achieved in Sunday schools. A Gloucester 'hemp and flax' manufacturer, a Mr Church, who employed 'great number' of Sunday school scholars, was asked by Raikes 'whether he perceived any alteration in the poor children' who worked for him and Raikes quoted his reply. ' "Sir," says he, "the change could not have been more extraordinary in my opinion, had they been transformed from the shape of wolves and tigers to that of men. In temper, disposition, and manners, they could hardly be said to differ from the brute creation. But since the establishment of the Sunday Schools, they have seemed anxious to shew that they are not the ignorant, illiterate creatures, they were before. When they have seen a superior come, and kindly instruct and admonish them, and sometimes reward their good behaviour, they are anxious to gain friendship and good opinion. They are also become more tractable and obedient, and less quarrelsome and revengeful. In short, I never conceived that a reformation so singular, could have been effected amongst the set of untutored beings I employed." '[5]

Education in Raikes' and Stock's Sunday schools was intended to train children to be orderly, tractable, submissive, industrious, pleasantly and kindly disposed, and respectful to their superiors.

Raikes strove earnestly to teach his scholars to be truthful and honest, with a view, of course, to preventing them from entering upon a life of crime. It was with some conceit that Raikes, in a business-cum-personal letter to his friend, the Revd W. Lewellyn of Leominster, informed him of the achievement in this aspect of education which he had pioneered. 'I have some satisfaction,' wrote Raikes on 11 July, 1792, 'in acquainting you that the State of this County is so much improved by the late Regulations, and the attention to the Improvement of morals among the common people, that we have not for the county one culprit to hold up his hand at the Bar of the next Assizes. A circumstance that the history of this County could never before record. The number about Ten years ago were from 50 to 100 that was usually tried. That was the period when Providence was pleased to make me the Instrument of introducing Sunday Schools and Regulations in Prisons.'

Teaching children to use acceptable, inoffensive speech called for patience and understanding. Admonition of the children who cursed and swore would bring but silence and sometimes sullen-

ness from the culprits. Encouraging poor, ignorant children to
avoid crudity and use speech more effectively could seldom be
accomplished quickly or easily. Nevertheless, through Raikes and
the Sunday schools, improved skills of communication were
acquired by increasing numbers of the sons and daughters of
common people.

Teaching of reading and spelling, which formed the chief intellectual content of the education provided in Raikes' and Stock's
Sunday schools, assisted the development of the children's powers of expression. Writing does not appear to have been included,
which is not surprising in view of the problems of supplying the
necessary desks, inkwells, ink, quill pens, and paper (sand trays
and slates and slate pencils were a later invention). To have found
anyone capable of teaching the children to write would also have
proved difficult. To the writing masters of the day writing meant
calligraphy – a complicated art, and the expense in furniture,
equipment, materials and salaries would have been prohibitive.
Neither Raikes nor Stock appear to have considered it. Other
early leaders in the movement have left their opinions. Sarah
Trimmer, after six years experience of running Sunday schools,
came to the conclusion that they should provide 'a sufficient portion of learning (excepting in the articles of writing and accounts,
a little of which one could wish all the poor might obtain though
the sabbath day is not a proper time for these acquirements) for
such cannot be spared on week-days from the labours of the
plough, or other occupations by which they contribute to the
support of families.'[6] Jonas Hanway was quite definite that writing was 'not of a nature proper to be taught to them, nor would it
be consistent, if it were, for the sabbath day'.[7] The ability to read
was necessary for religious reasons, the texts read in Sunday
schools being chiefly the scriptures and moral stories. But Raikes
did not restrict the teaching of reading to Sundays only.

He encouraged a new development: the provision of evening
classes on weekdays. This indicates Raikes' clear intention to
'educate' the children, not simply to habituate them into Sunday
routines. When he discovered that some children wanted more
instruction than could be provided on Sundays, and that the parents and other young women were anxious to join the classes, he
made provision for this. In 1784, Raikes wrote, 'To some of the
school-mistresses I give two shillings a week extra to take the

children when they come from work, during the week days.'[8]
And the next year he gave a further explanation of this in a letter
to William Fox: 'With respect to the possibility of teaching children, by the attendance they give upon the Sunday, I thought
with you, at my first onset, that little was to be gained; but I now
find that it has suggested to the parents, that the little progress
we made on the Sunday might be improved, and they have,
therefore, engaged to give the teacher a penny a-week, to admit
of the children, once or twice a day, during the recess from work,
at dinner time or evening, to take a lesson every day in the week.
To one of my teachers, who lives in the worst part of our suburbs,
I allow 2s a-week extra, (besides the shilling I give her for the
Sunday employ,) to let all that are willing come and read in this
manner. I see admirable effects from this addition to my scheme.
I find mothers of the children, and grown up young women, have
begged to be admitted to partake of this benefit. Sorry I am to
say, that none of the other sex have shewn the same desire.'[9]

Raikes noted the eagerness of children to learn to read and
besides their 'desire to be taught' it registered with him that
'many children began to show talents for learning'.[10] A similar
observation on ability shown by poor children was made by Jonas
Hanway: 'I have been told of a boy who learnt the alphabet in a
day; and I have heard a Sunday School girl of six years of age,
repeat the whole of a long chapter in the New Testament.'[11]
Through Raikes' enterprise, intelligent children of poor families
learned to read and to spell, to comprehend the written word, to
assimilate ideas, to express themselves, to reason and to question.
Wittingly or unwittingly, Raikes and the Sunday school teachers
gave thousands of common people a key to knowledge and
understanding.

It is doubtful whether Raikes' own ideas on popular education
were as advanced as those of Joseph Lancaster – a schoolmaster
later famous for popularising the monitorial school – who wrote
in 1803, that he wished to 'carry the system of education (for the
common people) to as high a pitch as possible'.[12] Raikes' reasons
for becoming involved in the work were different for, as we have
seen, these were his concern over the 'uncivilised behaviour' of
the poor children and his desire to prevent them taking to crime.
Furthermore, Raikes was not of the same humble beginnings as
Lancaster, and Raikes' views were in large measure influenced by

the conservative ones of his associates, entrepreneurs, clergymen, and local gentry. Raikes was a man of open mind, however, always ready to consider new ideas. He would not have objected, for instance, to supplying any poor person, who could afford the pence, with a copy of his newspaper. On the contrary, although there is no evidence of children in his Sunday school being supplied with newspapers, he would doubtless have welcomed a possible extension of his newspaper's future readership if the poor learned to read. Apart from business considerations Raikes, through his knowledge of the printing world, would appreciate the importance and power of the written word for everyone – rich and poor.

Raikes' outlook would probably have concurred with that of Richard Townley, who believed that the provision of education for the common people would result in great benefits to the national prosperity. 'It is generally allowed, that more ingenious improvements, and useful inventions in machinery,' wrote Townley in 1784, 'have taken their rise in these Northern parts' of the country where the nationally important cotton and woollen industries employed large numbers of people. Production in the mills had made great progress in a relatively short space of time thanks to new 'inventions and improvements' devised 'by such as are usually denominated the inferior ranks of mankind', who had 'by some means or other obtained a moderate share of learning' and therefore been enabled to apply their intelligence to increasing and improving productivity. 'If due encouragement is given . . . by affording greater numbers an opportunity of qualifying themselves,' argued Townley, then 'greater improvements, or inventions still more useful, may be reasonably expected. This consideration alone – were there not many others of a more exalted and generous nature – should be a strong inducement to adopt Mr Raikes's humane and excellent plan, or one nearly similar to it.'[13] Neither Townley nor Raikes appreciated the complexities of education or foresaw the tremendous social and political changes which must inevitably follow the spread of knowledge and enlightenment.

The growth of Sunday schools throughout the kingdom, as one historian described it, was 'a phenomenon in the history of education which is without parallel'.[14] Raikes' hopes for 'this effort at civilisation' were more than justified. In the half century following the commencement of Raikes' publicity of them in 1783, Sunday schools provided instruction for hundreds of thousands of children of labouring families. Sunday schools became a strong influence in factory communities in the early decades of the nineteenth century. 'In the new factory towns, amidst the social degradation and anarchy produced by violent economic change prolonged through twenty years of war, they (Sunday schools) were the sole organs of a community that transcended the fierce antagonism of misconceived class interests. In them the masters, foremen and workers of the factory met on the common ground of mutual service.'[15] Sunday schools, besides giving religious teaching to their scholars, were the chief agency for their secular education. Many poor but able children, having been taught the rudiments of reading and spelling in Sunday school, had the determination and persistence to obtain the literature, and such instruction as they could get, to educate themselves. Thus armed they fought for social and political recognition for themselves, their families and their neighbours.

Sunday schools having received universal acclaim, and confirmation having been given Raikes' assertion that 'the lower orders of mankind' were capable of improvement and that 'an attempt to reclaim them' was practicable, ideas, convictions and experiments to effect this proliferated in some variety. In Minchinhampton in 1784, children of destitute families were taught to spin wool and flax on weekdays and by their labours to help to support themselves. In addition, as suggested by Raikes, a Sunday school was established there. 'Working schools' or 'schools of industry' were not a new device. They had been advocated by John Locke, the seventeenth century philosopher, who had suggested that all children 'above three and under fourteen years of age', of families in receipt of relief from the parish should be fed at such schools.[16] In 1697 a 'working school for a hundred girls' had been established in a workhouse in Bristol.[17] Raikes applauded ideas like this and his newspaper carried an account of such an enterprise in Haverfordwest, South Wales. 'A gentleman of Coventry has purchased an estate in this county, is erecting spinning machines and has begun to employ the children of the poor; some of whom are already capable of earning their maintenance.'[18]

Mrs Sarah Trimmer was also an advocate of schools of industry, two of which she opened at Brentford in 1786, in the belief that 'by mixing labour with learning' the children become 'particularly eligible' afterwards 'to be employed in manufactures, and other inferior offices of life'.[19] She suggested the following employments for pupils in the schools: carding, spinning, knitting and needlework for the girls, and coarse thread spinning and sailmaking for the boys. The tuition envisaged was extremely limited: the girls, she thought, might be given some insight into domestic economy,[20] whilst the boys were to learn 'some of the lower mechanical arts'.[21] The ultimate object of her schools, as she declared it, was to be 'the improvement of morals'.[22]

Schools of industry received publicity from Raikes alongside that given to Sunday schools. On 9 July, 1787, he published a description of the anniversary celebrations of the establishment of Sunday schools in Cardiff, together with the following passages: 'The inhabitants (of Cardiff), encouraged by the change of manners of the children, are meditating an extension of their plan. – The ladies of the town, to their honour be it spoken, have raised a handsome subscription for the establishment of a "School of Industry," upon the plan set forth in Mrs Trimmer's *ECONOMY OF CHARITY*. The girls, who recommend themselves by their proper deportment at the Sunday School, are to be taught, during the week, sewing, knitting, spinning, and other such modes of employment, as may make them more useful in their several stations.' Raikes' correspondent also reported that 'a similar institution has been lately established by the ladies of Abergavenny, which promises the happiest effects'.[23]

At the end of the same month, from 'among many instances . . . of systematic attention to the lowest class', Raikes publicised 'a striking example' to be found in the town of Ledbury, Herefordshire. The workhouse building had been repaired to accommodate children employed in the manufacture of bags from raw hemp. The advantages were that the children from an early age became 'instrumental to their own maintenance' and 'being trained to order and industry . . . (were thereby) likely to turn out valuable members of the community, instead of vagabonds and plunderers'.[24]

Schools of industry were often set up to accommodate those Sunday school children not already employed on weekdays. On 7 January, 1788, the *Gloucester Journal* contained an account of the establishment of four Sunday schools in Cheltenham, to which 'about 100 of the most neglected children of the poor' had been admitted, and Raikes' correspondent there concluded with the prediction: 'The possibility of civilising these children, has encouraged us to think of establishing Schools of Industry, which is the completion of the plan. Before the summer expires, we flatter ourselves this point will be carried.'[25]

The Crown saw merit in such schools and Raikes made sure his readers knew of the Queen's well-doing. On 20 October, 1788, he published part of a letter he had received from Windsor: 'Her Majesty has established a school for spinning in a small house in Dachet-Lane, where a number of children are instructed in that art, and cloathed and supported by her royal bounty. A governess superintends the manual labour, and great care and attention are paid to the morals of the children. This is a laudable endeavour of our most gracious Queen, to promote habits of industry in the rising generation, and suppress those which bear a tendency to idleness and sloth. It may be said, that the children work under the immediate eye of Her Majesty, for she is a constant visitor to inspect the various process of the business, and to direct them in all their proceedings. – What an example is here held forth for the imitation of the British ladies.'[26]

Similar aims to those of Raikes for the education of the poor, except for some stringent reservations, were pursued by Hannah More, the religious writer, when she began her work in the Cheddar district.[27] Helped by her sisters, she responded to an appeal made by William Wilberforce to help the poor of that area. When on a visit to Cheddar, Wilberforce had been appalled by the ignorance, depravity and vice which he found there. He knew of the sisters' work in their Sunday schools at Churchill and Wrington and he discussed with them what might be done. After Wilberforce and his friends had offered to finance the establishment of schools in the area, the sisters extended their operations to cover several parishes in the Cheddar district and established both Sunday schools and 'day working schools', eight between 1789 and 1791, and four more before the end of the century.

Landowners of the Cheddar area were not easily convinced that it would be in their interest to support the establishment of the schools. The reaction of one important landowner was to beg Hannah More not to bring religion to the poor as it made them 'lazy and useless'.[28] Only when the idea was conveyed that fewer orchards would be robbed and less poultry stolen, because the children would be shut up in school, was the support of some of the farmers obtained. However, in spite of initial setbacks, in under five years the sisters had an attendance of two hundred children and the same number of adults.[29]

Hannah showed their schools to be a social force stronger than that of the magistracy and the law. She wrote: 'On Sunday was enabled to open the school. It was an affecting sight. Several of the grown-up youths had been tried at the last assizes; three were the children of a person lately condemned to be hanged, many thieves, all ignorant, profane and vicious beyond belief. Of this banditti we have enlisted one hundred and seventy; and when the clergyman, a hard man, who is also the magistrate, saw these creatures kneeling round us, whom he had seldom seen but to commit or punish in some way, he burst into tears.'[30]

The 'day working schools' of Cheddar appear to have resembled the schools of industry, but also to have had a strong religious bias. The boys engaged in raffia work, whilst the girls undertook sewing and needlework, but all the children were carefully instructed in religious knowledge and taught to read. Evening classes were held for the benefit of some of the adult poor.

Hannah More's views on the education of the poor were austere, and she admitted no change in their social position. In a letter to the Bishop of Bath and Wells, dated 1801, she wrote, 'My plan of instruction is extremely simple and limited. They learn, on weekdays, such coarse works as may fit them for servants. I allow no writing for the poor. My object is not to make fanatics, but to train up the lower classes in habits of industry and piety.'[31]

Changes recorded in the religious habits of the poor indicated the effectiveness of instruction. Whereas 'in the populous and extensive parish of Cheddar' the average attendance at the parish church numbered twenty in 1789 when the More sisters began their enterprise, ten years later the regular attenders were calculated to be over eight hundred.[32]

A fundamental difference can be found between the attitude of the More sisters and that of Raikes in respect of the education of the poor. Those ladies strove to inculcate pious humility and subordination in labouring class children, whilst Raikes, however brutal his disciplinary measures were on occasion, tried also to challenge the intelligence and elevate the minds of the children in his Sunday schools.

Schools of industry were established at various places in the country, for it was thought that by training the poor to be industrious, both pauperism and the cost of parish relief would be reduced. The arguments in favour of the establishments were that they provided opportunities for social, moral and religious training, and the children who normally worked in factories were removed from the unhealthy conditions which existed there, and also protected from the profanity and immorality exhibited by some of the adult workers.[33]

Pressure was sometimes brought to bear upon parents to send their children to the schools of industry. At a spinning school established at Oakham in 1787, for instance, the Poor Law Overseers forbade parish relief to those parents whose children did not attend such a school, unless they could be employed more advantageously elsewhere.[34] William Pitt in his proposals for Poor Law reform in 1796 tried to legislate for the compulsory attendance of children of parents in receipt of parish relief at schools of industry, but as this conflicted with the interests of mill owners who employed children, the idea was abandoned.

Establishment of a school of industry depended upon the ability of the organisers to sell commodities produced, and upon the inducements which could be used to persuade parents to allow their children to attend. Chiefly for these reasons schools of industry provided a limited measure of education for relatively few children. Parliamentary returns for 1803 recorded that of the 188,794 children between the ages of five and fourteen years whose parents were in receipt of parish relief only 20,336 attended schools of industry.[35]

A new innovation in charity education at Bath was publicised by Raikes in March, 1789[36] the 'plans' of which were being sold for sixpence a copy. The three types of charity school in the city were organised into a hierarchy. Sunday schools accommodated children who before their establishment were seen 'rioting in the streets and offending the inhabitants by their dirt and profaneness'.[37] Thirty Sunday schools, seventeen for girls and thirteen for boys, each with an enrolment of twenty-five children six years of age or over, were taught by a mistress or master and inspected by a lady or gentleman visitor. The children were taught their letters, to read and spell, to repeat individually the Catechism and an explanation of its meaning, and to say in unison the Lord's Prayer, the Creed, Confessions and Responses. They also attended services in the church. Rewards were given by visitors for progress and good behaviour and 'regular attendance for six months and good behaviour' qualified a child 'for being a candidate for the School of Industry: also for admittance into the Blue-Coat School, Margaret Chapel, and Queen-Square Chapel Schools, in each of which Schools they (were) cloathed and apprenticed afterwards'.[38]

The second type of charity school in Bath, the school of industry, was attended by one hundred and eighty children in the care of six mistresses, a matron, a weaver and a wool-comber. A variety of skills were taught: thirty little girls were taught to knit garters and stockings; thirty little boys were taught to knit garters and stockings and to make all sorts of nets; thirty girls and thirty boys were taught to spin wool for clothing and stockings and also to card wool; thirty girls were instructed in the spinning of flax to make their own linen; and thirty girls were taught to sew. The weaver wove the clothing and linen for clothes made for the children, whilst the wool-comber combed, washed and dyed the wool and worsted, and taught the spinning boys to read. He was also their Sunday school master.

The aims of the school of industry at Bath were clearly stated. It was hoped to teach the children employments which would be of use to themselves and enable them 'to earn their subsistence': in the case of girls to qualify them 'for apprentices or servants to mechanics, tradesmen, or farmers'.[39] The school founders thought that sewing was 'absolutely necessary for all females to know; thus a girl who has gone through the schools, will be able to prepare materials for her own clothing, make her own stockings, make up and mend her linen and clothes'.[40] The older girls also took it in turns to clean the house. In July, 1789 the Overseers of the Poor in the different parishes of Bath, at the request of the Committee for Conducting Sunday Schools, refused poor relief to parents unless their children attended Sunday schools.

Admission to a place in the third category, the older charity schools,[41] which had always been selective, became more so, and the status of these schools rose accordingly. The superior poor who attended charity schools were provided with weekday education of a higher standard and content than that of Sunday schools and schools of industry. As industry and commerce in the late eighteenth century increasingly required a labour force capable of reading, writing and cyphering and of casting accounts, the scholars leaving charity schools became eligible for skilled employment in mines, manufactories, and wholesale and retail trade.

A ladder of opportunity, short and narrow though it was, enabled a few children to climb a little higher socially, and to be rescued from a life of drudgery and impoverishment. The poor, as Raikes knew, could not do this unaided. The aforementioned Committee of Gentlemen at Bath were not the first, of course, in awarding places in charity schools to Sunday school scholars. Raikes, in publishing a report on the 'Anniversary Sermon' for the benefit of Sunday schools in Cirencester, quoted a statement that 'In the short period of the last twelve months, forty-eight children in this town, who before admittance into the Sunday School were in a state of total ignorance, have so distinguished themselves, that they have been apprenticed, taken into service, and placed out into superior charity schools.'[42]

All three types of charity supported school – Sunday schools, schools of industry, and the older established charity schools – were commended and encouraged by the Society for Bettering the Condition of the Poor. Founded in 1796 the Society received the patronage of George III. Under the presidency of the Bishop of Durham, branches were opened in various parts of the country. The Society's policy went further than just alleviating immediate distresses of the poor by providing food, blankets, etc, for it was hoped to educate the poor to help themselves. Thomas Bernard, its Vice-President, wrote in 1802, 'Of all means of soothing the distresses, improving the habits and encouraging the virtues of the poor, none will be found more gratifying, or more effectual, than a general impartial provision for the education of their children.'[43] An indication of the continued and universal influence of Raikes is evident in the same writer's work *Education of the Poor* published in 1809, in which Bernard pointed out that 'one of the greatest advantages' of day schools compared with boarding schools for poor children was 'the improvement of the other poor', and to illustrate this he used 'an interesting anecdote by Mr Raikes of Gloucester'.[44]

Public interest in the education of the poor having been aroused by Raikes and by the effectiveness of Sunday schools in changing the behaviour of their scholars, the crucial problem of how costs might be met to provide this education was frequently reviewed. The possibility that all children could receive some education, if only that provided by Sunday schools was, thanks to Raikes, generally accepted and was the beginning of universal education. The two great advantages of Sunday schools were that children could be employed on weekdays and that the schools could be run cheaply. The teachers in receipt of payment expected only emoluments usual to their low station and increasing numbers of unpaid teachers were undertaking the work. Also the money required to pay for the accommodation, heating and equipment was very small and could easily be raised. On the other hand, if the costs were minimal, so was the amount of instruction which could be given. Raikes and other Sunday school founders marvelled at what had been achieved in the education of their scholars at so little expense, but the limitations of Sunday school instruction were sensibly recognised.

Beilby Porteous, Bishop of Chester, contended that had charity schools been 'sufficiently general and extensive . . . (they) would in all probability have obviated a great part of the evils' of which people were complaining. 'But,' he wrote, 'the expence of founding and supporting them prevents them from becoming universal,' and he admitted, that 'In many towns, and by far the greatest number of villages, there are no Charity Schools at all.' Sunday schools were 'a very proper and useful appendage to them'.[45] Accurate estimates of the numbers of children attending endowed and subscription charity schools in the 1780's are not left to us, but one historian gave the figure of 30,000 in 1760.[46] Adamson, historian of education, stated, 'In the last year of the reign of George I (1727) charity schools existed in every county of England and Wales, Flint and Cardigan excepted, to the number of 1,389, teaching 22,024 boys and 5,830 girls.' He added also that 'with the accession of George III in 1760 . . . the (charity) schools dropped behind (population growth) both in number and in public usefulness.'[47]

Thomas Bernard suggested in 1809 some reasons for fewer scholars being admitted into SPCK schools. First the trustees said they preferred to board a few scholars than instruct many, because the morals of the pupils were being 'corrupted at home'. A more important reason was that 'a school which entirely supports a few (scholars) supplies useful patronage. If a servant's child is admitted, the parent can afford to be satisfied with less wages', and if a 'parish child' is boarded then 'the school endowment comes opportunely in aid of the parish rate'.[48] Bernard stated that the cost of maintaining and instructing a boy 'in a charity school was from twelve to eighteen guineas a year'.[49]

New charity schools were opened after 1760 and two of the staunchest supporters of Sunday schools helped to set up charity schools in Gloucestershire. William Fox established a charity school at Clapton. The Revd Samuel Glasse was one of the founders of Eastington Charity School. In 1784, along with eight other gentlemen, he contributed to an endowment, the interest from which gave support to the school. The Revd Richard Raikes 'furnished the premises' in Lower North-gate Street, Gloucester, of a school for two hundred poor boys. Raikes' brother's action enabled funds 'bequeathed (for this purpose) by Mrs Dorothy Cocks and John Hyett' to be used, and a master was engaged to instruct the scholars in 'reading, writing and accounts'. This 'ragged' school came under the management and 'direction of the Corporation and Guardians of the Poor'.[50] Raikes himself took an interest in the establishment of charity schools. When one was opened in Dymock in Gloucestershire in 1785 to 'extend the Blessings of Education to the Poor' by providing weekday instruction in 'reading, writing, and arithmetic' the body of subscribers to the school on 27 April, 1785 resolved 'that the thanks of this meeting be given to Mr Robt. Raikes for his benevolent assistance rendered on this occasion'.[51]

Raikes often published information about charity schools, sermons preached and collections made[52] and, of course, the occasions when a new one was opened, as at Ross in May, 1792. An endowment by a Walter Scott, after his death, provided the school with an annual sum of £200 'to cloathe and educate 30 boys and 20 girls'.[53] Charity schools, however, accommodated relatively few children at this time of population growth: 40,000 was given by one writer as the number of children attending charity schools in 1792.[54]

Meanwhile the Sunday schools had an ever-widening appeal and clergy and laymen all over the country expressed their belief in this simplistic solution for curing social ills. Sarah Trimmer wrote in 1792 that she had been informed that 500,000 children attended Sunday schools.[55] Raikes could be hopeful that most of the nation's children would eventually receive 'education', if only on Sundays, and would be taken to church.

Events at the end of the eighteenth century changed the attitude of many of the governing classes towards the labouring classes. The ameliorative schemes of the philanthropists were greatly influenced by the political tensions of the time. Revolutionary ideas and opposition to them had their reaction upon the education of the poor. The French Revolution made an impact on this country. Before this event the ruling classes, generally speaking, had regarded the mass of the labouring population as a passive part of the community, but after observing the events across the Channel, they now appeared as a possible political danger. English newspapers reported the horrors of the French Revolution and warned their readers of the terrible deeds committed by upholders of the Jacobin doctrines.

The French Revolution split the Whig Party. Charles James Fox, the Whig Leader, enthusiastically approved of the French Revolution, while other Whigs thought it bore a resemblance to their own 'glorious revolution' of 1688. Dr Richard Price, a Unitarian minister and leader of great influence among middle class dissenters who met in the 'revolutionary clubs' welcomed the French Revolution. Small and large societies for reform were inspired by the French Revolution. Some were selective dining clubs, and the annual subscription for their members ran into guineas. Others, like the London Corresponding Society, collected a weekly subscription of one penny from their members and were overwhelmingly supported by common people – artisans and small tradesmen.

Edmund Burke voiced the change which was to come in Whig opinion. One of the greatest thinkers of the Whig Party, Burke published in November, 1790, his *Reflections on the French Revolution* in which he decried the measures taken, their consequences and, worst of all, what he saw as their dreadful example. Burke's views made a profound impression and aroused opinion against the Revolution. Thomas Paine replied to Burke's attack on the French Revolution with his *Rights of Man* published 1791–2. Paine's writings provided much of the inspiration for the reform movement in Britain. The Corresponding Societies from their centres in large towns circulated Paine's *Rights of Man*, along with pamphlets and newspaper cuttings.

Paine (1737–1809), a former stay-maker, exciseman, and soldier, applied his mind to the problem of property and the economics of state provision of popular education. He was among the first of the common people to argue politics with his own class. Raikes and the Sunday schools had begun religious, moral and intellectual enlightenment of the masses, but through Paine came new political ideas. 'Mankind are not now to be told they shall not think or they shall not read;' he declared, 'and publications that go no further than to investigate principles of government, to invite men to reason and reflect and to shew the errors and excellencies of different systems, have a right to appear.'[56] Paine knew the suffering of the poor: 'age going to the workhouse and youth going to the gallows',[57] and he asked, 'Why is it that scarcely any are executed but the poor?' and replied to his own question, 'The fact is a proof, among other things, of a wretchedness in their condition. Bred up without morals, and cast upon the world without a prospect, they are the exposed sacrifice to vice and legal barbarity.'[58] He set out clearly, in plain English, ideas for social reform, showing that the country could afford child allowances (£4 for each child of poor families) and old-age pensions (to commence at 50 and increased at 60).[59] He said that the State should become responsible for the education of every child of a poor family and that the children should 'learn reading, writing and common arithmetic'. Also for those families 'not properly of the class of the poor' he advocated an allowance of 'ten shillings a year for the expense of schooling for six years each, which will give them six months' schooling each year, and half a crown a year for paper and spelling books'.[60]

As a Christian, Raikes' appeal was to the heart of the individual; as a democrat, Paine levelled his argument against the heart of the social constitution. 'A nation under a well-regulated government should permit none to remain uninstructed. It is monarchical and aristocratical government only that requires ignorance for its support.'[61] The aims of Thomas Paine for the common people were very like those of Raikes. 'When it shall be said by any country in the world,' wrote Paine, 'my poor are happy; neither ignorance nor distress is to be found among them;

my jails are empty of prisoners, my streets of beggars, the aged are not in want; the taxes are not oppressive; the rational world is my friend, because I am a friend of its happiness: When these things can be said, then may that country boast its constitution and its government.'[62] On ways of achieving these aims their respective outlooks were very different.

Raikes, even though he held strong convictions about an Englishman's rights such as the freedom of the press, would never have been a party to the political radicalism of Paine. Raikes' pioneering, however, was to assist in furthering the reforms advocated by Paine, because Sunday schools made a valuable beginning in the development of 'popular intelligence and intellect' while Paine's simple logic was to provide encouragement and hope to those classes who were permitted no political voice.

The majority of Whigs and Tories agreed with Burke's view that the French Revolution was an anarchical movement. Reports of the September massacres in Paris, when hundreds of people were barbarously murdered because of their suspected hostility to the Revolution, shocked and sickened many of its English supporters. These and subsequent events made people in England, as one newspaper put it, 'reflect with gratitude upon the peace and good order, which, emanating from our Happy Constitution, prevail at home'.[63] In towns throughout the country citizens attended meetings to prove their loyalty to the existing Constitution. Raikes attended a meeting of the mayor, citizens and inhabitants of Gloucester at which those present declared their 'Loyalty and Attachment to our King and Veneration for the British Constitution' and he was one of the sixty knights, clergy and gentlemen who were appointed to 'consult and adopt such particular measures as the exigency of affairs may from time to time require'.[64] In December, 1792, Thomas Paine was prosecuted by the British Government (in his absence) and found guilty of writing and publishing libel, the 'seditious book' being the Second Part of *Rights of Man*.

To counter revolutionary ideas, which circulated among the common people, the ruling classes encouraged public ridicule of Paine. Raikes published accounts of, as he put it, 'expressions of detestation for Paine and his principles', the occasion at Birdlip, near Gloucester, being typical of those which took place in 'most other towns and villages in the country'. The inhabitants of Bird-lip 'being actuated with the truest spirit of loyalty, zeal and attachment to our most gracious Sovereign and happy Constitution, prepared a figure to resemble Tom Paine; which being judiciously equipped with a pair of old stays under one arm, the *Rights of Man* under the other, and a halter round his neck was put in a cart and drawn about the village by a mangy horse, attended by a select band of music, playing God save the King; and several persons, with guns, who marched in military order after the cart and fired many distinct vollies during the procession; after which he was taken to the gallows erected, on the summit of the hill where he was hanged and shot amidst the acclamations of a vast concourse of people. An immense pile of faggots, which was placed under the gallows being set on fire, poor Thomas was in a short time reduced to ashes . . . the evening was concluded in the greatest harmony, loyalty and good order.'[65] It is easy to imagine the sentiments Raikes would have engendered, at this time, in his Sunday school scholars.

Hannah More responded to many appeals that she should produce some simple literature which catered for labouring class readers and which would provide an antidote to the allegedly 'poisonous writings' of Tom Paine. One of the most widely read of these tracts was *Village Politics*, which Hannah published in 1792 under the pseudonym Will Chip. In this tract, through the character of Jack Anvil, a village blacksmith, she derided Tom Paine and his book *Rights of Man* and extolled the virtue of the British constitution. When *Village Politics* first appeared in print, its usefulness to their cause was immediately recognised by the Tories. Many individuals had large editions printed at their own expense, and the Government sent thousands of copies to Scotland and Ireland.

War with France broke out at the beginning of 1793. The political atmosphere of the country was charged with fear of insurrection. The army was alerted and new units established. William Pitt, the Prime Minister, believed that if he resigned he would suffer a fate similar to that of the late French monarch. The eighteenth century practice of lodging troops with the civilian population was discontinued. It was considered a dangerous practice, especially in the manufacturing towns. Pitt pursued a policy of building barracks, where the troops could be under the constant

surveillance of their officers. Following the advent of the war the
government regarded Radicals who criticised its policy or the constitution as traitors, and severe measures were taken to repress
them. The *Habeas Corpus Act* was suspended in 1794. Numbers of
men, against whom there was no evidence, were kept in prison
for years. The *Treasonable Practices Act* became law in 1795. This
made writing, printing, and speaking or in any way inciting
against the sovereign, government, or constitution a serious
offence. Also in the same year the *Seditious Meetings Act* prohibited public meetings unless licensed by a magistrate, and most
magistrates considered meetings for discussion of reform illegal.
Stamp and advertisement duties were increased to stop the publication of cheap newspapers, and new regulations were imposed
upon the press. Under a law, which classified reading-rooms and
unlicensed debating clubs as brothels, the London Corresponding
Society and other societies were suppressed. By the *Combination
Acts* of 1799 and 1800 working men were forbidden to form Trade
Unions for fear they should be 'revolutionary'.[66] Repression and
coercion were policies the ruling classes considered right to pursue.

Fear and suspicion were sometimes reflected in attitudes
towards the Sunday schools and charity schools. Altruistic work,
particularly in nonconformist schools, became suspect as being
unpatriotic and dangerous. William Pitt, it has been alleged,
thought seriously about introducing a Bill to suppress Sunday
schools.[67] An anonymous correspondent using the signature
'Eusebius' had his letter, which was highly critical of Sunday
schools, published in the October, 1797 edition of the *Gentleman's
Magazine*. The writer was of the belief that 'the fear of the gallows
operates more strongly on the multitude than the fear of God'.
His argument was the very antithesis of that of Raikes. 'There are,
perhaps,' Eusebius wrote, 'more criminals among that class of
men who have had a superficial education than among those who
have never been taught either to write or read. The laborious
occupations of life must be performed by those who have been
born in the lowest stations; but no one will be willing to undertake the most servile employment, or the meanest drudgery, if his
mind is opened, and his abilities increased, by any tolerable share
of scholastic improvement: yet these employments and this
drudgery must be necessarily performed. Society cannot possibly

subsist without them; and, surely, none can be more properly fitted for this purpose than those who have been born in a state of poverty. The man, whose mind is not illuminated by one ray of science, can discharge his duty in the most sordid employment without the smallest views of raising himself to a higher station, and can take his rest at night in perfect satisfaction and content. His ignorance is a balm that soothes his mind into stupidity and repose, and excludes every emotion of discontent, pride, and ambition. A man of no literature will seldom attempt to form insurrections, or plan an idle scheme for the reformation of the State. Conscious of his inability, he will withdraw from such associations; while those who are qualified by a tincture of superficial learning, and have imbibed the pernicious doctrines of seditious writers, will be the first to excite rebellions, and convert a flourishing kingdom into a state of anarchy and confusion.' Sunday schools, he concluded, were 'subversive of that order, that industry, that peace and tranquility which constitute the happiness of society.'

The most loyal subjects, if concerned with the education of the poor, were sometimes the objects of distrust. Hannah More, for instance, complained to her bishop in 1801 that one of her schools was charged with having prayed for the success of the French in the war, and she herself maligned. Of the pamphlets denouncing her she wrote, 'I am accused of being an abettor, not only of fanaticism and sedition, but of thieving and prostitution.'[68] As far as is known, no one, during his lifetime, ever maligned Raikes. The soundness of Raikes' judgement in proposing Sunday instruction as a means of improving the lot of the poor, and his suggestion that the clergy and the well-to-do should become involved and ultimately responsible for this, was demonstrated by the continued expansion of the Sunday School Movement. Paine's ideas, however profound the impression created upon thinking men of radical mind, produced severe reactionary measures on the part of the ruling classes, and his arguments about men's rights were not to prove, at this time, as beneficial to the poor as Raikes' appeals for charity.

Another advocate of State provision for the education of the poor, the Revd Thomas Robert Malthus (1766–1834) propounded an argument diametrically opposite to that of Paine, but one in which he approached the problem in a totally different way from

Raikes. Dr Malthus, concerned for the suffering poor, investigated the problem of population growth and in 1798 published his work *An Essay on the Principles of Population as it affects the Future Improvement of Society*. The scholarly doctor, a happily married man with eleven daughters, knew the power of the sex drive, and whilst agreeing that 'the passion between the sexes is necessary',[69] contended that 'Population, when unchecked, increases in a geometrical ratio (2,4,8,16,32) (and) subsistence increases only in an arithmetical ratio (2,3,4,5,6,7).'[70]

The 'preventive and the positive checks' on population increase, he declared, were misery and vice – in other words, 'the want of proper and sufficient food . . . hard labour and unwholesome habitations . . . vicious customs with respect to women, great cities, unwholesome manufactures, luxury, pestilence, and war'.[71] Malthus deprecated the system of poor relief, because he contended that the immense sums which were ravished on the poor tended to aggravate rather than alleviate their difficulties. Malthus believed that if people were given more food, then they would have more children, and poverty was therefore inevitable unless the poor could be persuaded to be prudent in increasing their families. He argued, 'It is not the duty of a man simply to propagate his species, but to propagate virtue and happiness, and that, if he has not a tolerably fair prospect of doing this, he is by no means called upon to leave descendants.'[72] Restraint by the labouring classes was the only alternative to an increase in population more rapid than an increase could be provided in means for their subsistence.

Malthus not only recommended State interference in education, but also complained that it was a national disgrace that the education of the lower classes 'should be left entirely to a few Sunday Schools'. He said that, 'In their education and in the circulation of those most important political truths that most nearly concern them, which are perhaps the only means in our power of really raising their condition and of making them happier men and more peaceful subjects, we have been miserably deficient.'[73]

To the editor of the *Gloucester Journal* parliamentary measures designed to ameliorate social ills were to be applauded. Raikes was prepared to sign a petition to local MP's to stop the misuse of grain, but he relied on Christian benevolence to meet the inequalities and adversities of life within the local community and to effect such reforms as the provision of popular education. The wisdom of his approach at the time is demonstrated by the attempts of others to involve Parliament in the education of the poor.

In the year of Raikes' retirement as proprietor and editor of the *Gloucester Journal*, 1802, Parliament first showed interest in the social education of the lower orders, when an Act for the *Preservation of Health and Morals of Apprentices and Others, employed in Cotton and Other Mills, and in Cotton and Other Factories* was passed. Members of the Manchester Board of Health were concerned in this measure. Sir Robert Peel – a friend of Dr Thomas Percival who founded the Manchester Board of Health in 1796 – and Robert Owen, a member of the Board, were both successful cotton manufacturers and aware of the ignorance and cruelty which existed in industry, and the Act was an attempt to prevent some of the abuses of child labour, and to ensure that the apprentices received some moral and religious education. Sir Robert Peel offered an educational reason for introducing his Bill: 'The great and first object I had in view in bringing in this Bill was to promote the religious and moral education of the children.'[74] The employers were expected to pay for the services of a master or mistress and provide a classroom where reading, writing and arithmetic could be taught. Every Sunday, for the space of at least one hour, apprentices were to be instructed in the Christian religion by a person of a denomination acceptable to the apprentices' parents.

The Act proved unworkable. Although it provided for factory inspectors appointed by JP's at the midsummer sessions, the proposed system of inspection was extremely difficult to carry out due to the remoteness of some of the mills and the ease with which the regulations could be ignored. However, if implementation of the Act proved impracticable, passing of it indicated that Members of Parliament conceived the State as an authority accepting responsibility for the education of some of the children of the labouring classes.

Samuel Whitbread, a Whig reformer, in February, 1807 declared his intention of presenting a Bill to deal with the problem of Poor Relief, and stated that the education of the pauper children was to form an important part of the measures proposed. He argued that nearly one seventh of the population was then receiving Poor Relief, and he expressed his concern over the rise in the amount of money spent on this: the sum had nearly doubled, he said, in the ten years before 1803.[75] Education, he thought, could achieve much more for much less. In his opinion the labourer could be educated 'so as to make him independent of his fellow creatures for his livelihood'.[76]

On 17 April in the same year, Whitbread introduced his *Parochial Schools Bill* which proposed a national system of elementary education by establishment of rate-aided parochial schools. All children of the poor were to be provided with two years' free schooling: reading, writing and arithmetic were to be the chief subjects in the curriculum; girls were to be given instruction in knitting and needlework. He said of this, 'In the adoption of a system of education, I forsee an enlightened peasantry, frugal, industrious, sober, orderly, contented: because they are acquainted with the true value of frugality, sobriety, industry and order. Crimes diminishing because the enlightened understanding abhors crime. The practice of Christianity prevailing, because the mass of your population can read, comprehend, and feel its divine origin, and the beauty of the doctrines which it inculcates.'[77] All this was possible, he thought, at a cost of five shillings per annum per child, if the method of teaching used by Joseph Lancaster (and earlier introduced by Raikes into his Sunday schools) were applied.

Whitbread's Bill raised the question (to which the nation, following Raikes' lead, had already answered in the affirmative) of whether it was desirable for the labouring classes to be educated at all. The Chancellor of the Exchequer, Spencer Percival, said that the kind of education proposed by Whitbread would not make the workers more industrious, religious or moral.[78] George Henry Rose, MP for Southampton, said that the working classes should be taught to read, but that he had some doubt about the desirability of their being taught to write. His opinion was, 'Those who learn to write well were not willing to abide to the plough.'[79]

Concern was expressed for the internal security of the country. In 1807 the war with France was still in progress and the adversary was the much feared Napoleon Bonaparte. These factors were significant in the arguments against the *Parochial Schools Bill*. Davies Giddy, MP for Bodmin, thought that the education of the labouring classes would cause discontent among them. He argued, 'However specious in theory the project might be of giving education to the labouring classes of the poor, it would, in effect be found to be prejudicial to their morals and happiness; it would teach them to despise their lot in life, instead of making them good servants of agriculture, and other laborious employments to which their rank in society had destined them; instead of teaching them subordination, it would render them refractory, as was evident in the manufacturing counties; it would enable them to read seditious pamphlets, vicious books, and publications against Christianity . . . The legislature would find it necessary to direct the strong arm of power towards them, and to furnish the executive magistrate with much more vigorous laws than were now in force.'[80] Whitbread was successful in piloting his Bill through the Commons, but the Lords threw it out on its second reading.

Although Parliament, in 1807, refused to accept responsibility for universal, gratuitous education of the poor, after the endeavours of Raikes, advocacy of it continued to gain strength. Never again, after these endeavours, did the cause of popular education lack an influential champion. Henry (Lord) Brougham, the Scottish Parliamentarian of powerful oratory, expansive knowledge and extraordinary ability to recall facts, succeeded Samuel Whitbread, and became its new, courageous, enthusiastic advocate. And with each new generation, fresh champions arose. Raikes had shown education to be the most effective social disciplinary force. He had also demonstrated that among the poor was a tremendous potential for good, and Richard Townley had observed that among the common people were minds capable of remarkable inventiveness, from which, if they were educated, the whole nation might benefit. From the ranks of the common people, the former pupil of a dissenting charity school, came a schoolmaster, Joseph Lancaster, who took the lead in popularising weekday education for the poor in the early decades of the nineteenth century. Raikes' ideas were still in evidence even when he no longer ran a newspaper and his pen had ceased to serve the cause of popular education. Sir James Kay Shuttleworth, the chief architect of elementary education in the nineteenth century could, with justification, write, 'The Sunday School was the root from which sprang our system of day schools.'[81]

The system Raikes had used in teaching prisoners in Gloucester Gaol to read, that of encouraging those who had mastered the skill to instruct others, was to prove the breakthrough in finding an economical means of providing popular education. Raikes instituted this system in his Sunday schools, appointing able children as 'leaders', who, under the supervision of the teacher, taught the other children. He described this system of organisation as follows: 'Twenty (children) is the number allotted to each teacher; the sexes kept separate. The twenty are divided into four classes. The children who show any superiority in attainments are placed as leaders of the several classes, and are employed in teaching others their letters, or hearing them read in a low whisper, which may be done without interrupting the master or mistress in their business, and will keep the attention of the children engaged, that they do not play, or make a noise.'[82]

The Revd Andrew Bell and Joseph Lancaster popularised the system. Bell appears to have been struck suddenly with the same idea shortly after taking over the post of superintendent of the Madras Male Orphan Asylum in 1789. He overcame the difficulty of teaching there by choosing clever boys to replace the inefficient teaching staff. On his return to England in 1797 he published a pamphlet entitled *An Experiment in Education at the Asylum at Madras*, and he introduced his system into St Botolph's Charity School, Aldgate, the schools of industry at Kendal, and the Bishop of Durham's 'Barrington School' at Bishop Auckland.

Joseph Lancaster, a Calvinistic, upright young man of scanty education, began in 1796, at the age of eighteen, to teach in a lower class district of London.[83] The numbers of his pupils increased and in 1801 he opened his school in a large room in Borough Road. Unable to afford a paid assistant, Lancaster appointed his more intelligent pupils as monitors to help with the teaching, and so devised a 'monitorial system' of school organisation upon which he elaborated as his school expanded. Lancaster who said that he 'was desirous of gaining information and instruction from a venerable man of seventy-two, who had superintended the education of 3,000 children', visited Raikes in 1808.[84] When advertising his school, Lancaster proferred arguments of which Raikes would have approved. 'Reading,' said Lancaster, 'multiplies the power of getting at the opinions and arguments of others. In the end, the good and sound arguments prevail.' Education, he declared, 'rendered the lower classes more tractable and less ferocious'.[85]

Voluntary supported day schools, organised on the monitorial system, rapidly increased in number in the second decade of the nineteenth century. Lancaster started the movement. His Borough Road establishment received the patronage of the King, the Royal Family, the Duke of Bedford and of Lord Somerville. During the years 1809 and 1810, as a result of Lancaster's lecture tours, ninety-five new schools accommodating 25,500 children were established and the Royal Lancasterian Association was formally instituted in 1810.

The Anglicans could not long remain unmoved by the success of the Royal Lancasterian Association in opening new schools. The time appeared to be critical, because to maintain its ascendancy as the Established Church steps had to be taken to protect its membership. A meeting, under the chairmanship of the Archbishop of Canterbury, held on 16 October, 1811, resulted in the establishment of the 'National Society for the Education of the Poor, throughout England and Wales, in the Principles of the Established Church'.[86] Assisted by the resources of the Church, the National Society founded schools throughout the kingdom. Charles Manners-Sutton, the Archbishop of Canterbury, became one of the Society's staunchest supporters, the Prince Regent became the patron, and the Dukes of York, Cambridge and Gloucester were among the first subscribers. The two great universities donated five hundred pounds each, and a fund amounting to several thousands of pounds was quickly raised.

Bishops, peers, clergy and laity supported the enterprise and provisional branches of the Society were established. The opening of the first National School in Gloucester, although Raikes did not live to see it, is of interest, not only because the provision of weekday education for the children of poor families would have received his approval, but because its establishment, and indeed the establishment of other National Schools in Gloucestershire, had more than a general connection with Raikes. Henry Ryder, the first Evangelical Bishop in England, consecrated Bishop of Gloucester in July, 1815, took a special interest in popular education, perhaps as a result of the influence of two of his friends, both of whom had special relationships with Raikes, one as a friend and the other as a distant relative. Ryder, during his office as Bishop, continued to enjoy the company of Hannah More at her home in Barley Wood, near Wells, and of William Wilberforce in London. In August, 1816 Henry Ryder took the chair at the inaugural meeting in Gloucester of the Gloucester Diocesan Society for the Education of the Poor in the Principles of the Established Church.[87] The Duke of Wellington laid the foundation stone on the London Road site of the first National School in Gloucester on 3 August, 1816. The Bishop in his address of thanks to the Iron Duke expressed his hopes for the work of the new school when he said, 'that arm which has been so long engaged in quelling tyrants and rearing up an unrivalled edifice of military fame, has been here, less brilliantly indeed, but very usefully employed in laying the foundation of a building calculated to prove the seminary of every private and social virtue'.[88] Such was the zeal of the supporters over the country that, after the National Society had been in existence only two years, it was claimed that two hundred and thirty schools had been opened accommodating 40,484 pupils, and that places were provided for over double that number by 1816.[89]

The committee of the Royal Lancasterian Society included members of both influence and stature: The Duke of Bedford, Henry Brougham, James Mill, Sir Samuel Romilly, Samuel Whitbread, William Wilberforce (Vice President) and William Allen. After continued irresponsibility by Lancaster in financial matters, he resigned, and the Royal Lancasterian Association became known in 1814 as the British and Foreign School Society. Local branches of the Society were established and with nonconformist support British Schools spread quickly across the country.

Reading, writing and arithmetic were included in the curricula of National and British Schools and, although the standard achieved by the scholars in these schools was very limited, there was now no question of preventing 'the diffusion of knowledge'. Voluntary effort, for which Raikes had appealed in the 1780's and 1790's, commenced the provision of popular education before the State accepted the responsibility.

Raikes' influence extended beyond English borders. In his newspaper he publicised both Sunday schools and Schools of Piety in Wales. 'Circulating schools' for the Welsh poor had been established by the Revd Griffith Jones in 1737. These schools were free, catechetical charity schools where the labouring poor, adults and children, were taught to read the Bible in Welsh. Bridget Bevan took over the organisation and management of the schools when the Revd Griffith Jones died in 1761 and continued this work until her death in 1779. A tribute to her was published by Raikes in 1780, and in concluding this it was noted that Mrs Bevan's son was undertaking responsibility for the schools. 'All letters relating to the Welsh Charity Schools are to be directed to Zacharias Bevan, Esq., . . . to who Mrs Bevan has committed the future care of them.'[90] Unfortunately the relatives contested her will and the £10,000 left by Mrs Bevan 'was invested in the Court of Chancery'[91] for thirty-one years. Without her leadership and financial support the circulating schools quickly declined and the organisation broke up.

The Revd Thomas Charles of Bala revived the circulating schools in 1785, but Sunday schools were preferred and were gradually established throughout the principality. The famous fifty mile walk from Llanfihangel to Bala and back by Mary Jones, the sixteen year old Welsh girl, who had carefully saved the money she had earned to purchase a Bible, Charles' endeavours to obtain Bibles printed in Welsh, and the subsequent founding of the British and Foreign Bible Society, were all expressions of the prevailing determination and pioneering spirit among the Welsh.

Richard Lovell Edgeworth (1744–1817), father of Maria Edgeworth the novelist, an Irishman of independent means, was well known in literary and scientific circles and represented a section of middle class opinion in the Irish Parliament. Author of *Practical Education*, an influential work containing carefully recorded observations about his own children, Edgeworth served on a board inquiring into Irish education from 1806 to 1811. Edgeworth was sufficiently conversant with Raikes' work to make reference to it in his correspondence. In his letter to Dr William Stuart, Protestant Lord Primate of Ireland, Edgeworth stated that 'it must always be a sufficient answer to those, who object to teaching the rudiments of knowledge to the poor, that of three thousand boys, who have been educated at the Sunday Schools in Gloucester, only ONE has been convicted of crime'.[92]

The provision of weekday schools did not halt the rapid growth of Sunday schools across the country. Even in August, 1788, the Sunday School Society Committee's report published by Raikes stated that 'In the various parishes of the kingdom, the number of poor children now attended to on Sundays amounts to as is said little less than 300,000'[93] and by thirty years later had almost doubled. The founding of the Sunday School Union by William Brodie Gurney in 1803 increased the impetus of the establishment of Sunday schools. Abstracted figures from various parliamentary returns (given to the nearest quarter million) show that the numbers of Sunday school children were 'half a million in 1818 and one and a half million in 1833; two and a half millions in 1851; five and three quarter millions in 1887; (and) seven and a half millions in 1898.'[94] Impressive as these figures are for the second half of the nineteenth century, it is those for the first half which have greater importance in respect of the provision of popular education, because for large numbers of children the only education they received was at Sunday school. Sunday schools had an advantage over the early day schools, however, in the length of the children's school life. If judged by Whitbread's expectations children attended weekday schools for two years, whereas, if only for one day a week, children were admitted to Sunday schools between six and twelve years of age, and many children not only attended for six years, but joined senior classes and became Sunday school teachers.

The significance of Raikes in the field of popular education was not necessarily as a visionary, foreseeing what Sunday schools might achieve. On his own admission he was at first very apprehensive as to whether the schools founded by Stock and himself would achieve anything at all. It was the sheer success of these schools after their inception which made him realise their potential rather than any hopes or intentions he may have had originally. What should be attributed to Raikes is the practicability of his ideas, and his thorough comprehension of what would be acceptable and what was likely to work. He acted as a human catalyst because his ideas coincided exactly with those of the wealthy who could be persuaded to support Sunday schools and those of the poor who could be persuaded to send their children to them.

To evaluate the importance of Raikes' work consideration should be given to the vast numbers of children who would otherwise have received no education of any kind, unless or until someone else had popularised the idea. Raikes' insistence upon cleanliness not only helped protect Sunday school scholars' health, but occasioned for them a psychological experience. The moment the child washed, he gained self-respect, in spite of his ragged clothes. Raikes' emphasis on teaching children to read, which, of course, few would have pursued to a high level of proficiency, gave to those with sufficient ability and determination a freedom to enter new dimensions of life. Raikes rewarded competence in reading. It is said that he requested the father of a boy to bring his son to his office with the promise that if he could read a chapter of the Testament which he (Raikes) specified, he would present him with a Bible – an expensive gift at this time. The child, who was not very tall, stood on a stool at Raikes' desk and read the first chapter of St Matthew's gospel, upon the completion of which Raikes gave him the Bible and made the request that he should not forget to read it.[95]

Perhaps most important of all, a child learned by attending Sunday school to converse with his neighbour and, of course, when he was able to communicate his own ideas, he acquired for himself that essential in the development of his personality, an identity. Raikes, probably having read the celebrated works of his uncle, John Clarke, the late headmaster of Hull Grammar School, understood the importance of mental training. The Sunday school founder certainly commended the sermon preached for the benefit of Sunday schools in St Mary de Crypt Church, Gloucester, by the Revd Dr Booker, who (to use Raikes' words) 'impressed the audience with so strong a sense of importance of mental cultivation in the rising offspring of the poor'.[96] For hundreds of children in Gloucester and perhaps, if only indirectly, hundreds of thousands of children throughout the kingdom, Raikes provided education by which to live.

In his 'reformation of society' Raikes did much more than this. He led clergy and laity back to the teachings of the Christian religion. With the advent of the Sunday schools clergy sought new texts, preached new sermons, and began to teach the children of the poor. Raikes wished to involve all ranks of society in the work of the Sunday schools. In his reply to William Fox's letter describing the first anniversary of Colchester Sunday School Raikes wrote, 'Instead of training horses to the course, and viewing with delight their exertions at Newmarket, let our men of fortune turn their eyes to an exhibition like that at Colchester. Impart with them a small portion of that solid enjoyment, which a mind like

yours must receive from the glorious sight. Children, more neglected than the beasts of the field, now taught to relish the comfort and decency, and good order, and to know that their own
happiness greatly depends on promoting the happiness of others.
When the community begins to reap the benefit of these principles, let us hope this nation will manifest to the world the blessed
effects of a general discussion of Christianity.'[97] After informing
the Revd Bowen Thickens of the Queen's desire that others
should follow the example of the ladies of fashion at Windsor
who taught in Sunday schools, Raikes wrote, 'You may mention
it to the ladies of Ross, who will not then, perhaps, be above
noticing the children of their poor neighbours, if they are present.'[98]

Sunday schools were attended by children of all sorts and conditions of common people: labourers, mill workers, factory workers, artisans and traders. They became a common meeting ground
for the poor and the rich, for the employees and the employers.
Sunday schools sometimes brought a little culture. Raikes often
reported musical items performed during special Sunday school
occasions, 'a select band (playing) several pieces of music'[99] and
'one of Mr Handel's coronation anthems (being) introduced'.[100]

To raise the poor from their state of ignorance and degradation
was the work of Sunday school teachers, and if the teachers were
recruited from the ranks of the common people it followed that
persons of higher education were needed to help and guide them.

For teacher and learners the labour would often be mutually
enlightening and rewarding. To a few, perhaps, came the realisation that we live to be educated. Through Raikes, a pioneer of
popular education, came the growth of Sunday schools. Through
Sunday schools many had life, and had it more abundantly.

NOTES

[1] Anon, *Sunday Schools Recommended as a Religious Institution. Sunderland Pamphlets, Religious* Vol I 1790
[2] Raikes, *Letter* 5 July, 1794
[3] *Gloucester Journal* 29 November, 1784
[4] Ibid 19 June, 1786
[5] Raikes, *Letter* 5 June, 1784
[6] Sarah Trimmer, *Reflections upon the Education of Children in Charity Schools* (1792)
pp 11, 12

[7] Jonas Hanway, *A Comprehensive View of Sunday Schools* (1786) p 30

[8] Raikes, *Letter* 5 June, 1784

[9] Ibid 20 June, 1785

[10] Ibid 5 June, 1784

[11] Hanway, op cit p 27

[12] J. Lancaster, *Improvements in Education* (1803) p 25

[13] *Leeds Intelligencer* 13 January, 1784

[14] Frank Smith, *A History of English Elementary Education* (1931) p 65

[15] George Unwin, *Samuel Oldknow and the Arkwrights* (1924) p 41

[16] R. H. Quick, *Some Thoughts Concerning Education by John Locke* (1889) Appendix A

[17] Brian Simon (editor), *Education in Leicestershire 1540–1940* (1968) p 60

[18] *Gloucester Journal* 26 September, 1785

[19] Trimmer, op cit p 11

[20] Sarah Trimmer, *The Economy of Charity* (1787) p 71

[21] Ibid p 119

[22] Ibid p 121

[23] *Gloucester Journal* 9 July, 1787

[24] Ibid 30 July, 1787

[25] Ibid 7 January, 1788

[26] Ibid 20 October, 1788

[27] It seems very probable that Hannah More was very well acquainted with Raikes' approaches and that the Raikes and the More sisters were friends.

[28] Hannah More, Letter to William Wilberforce 1789; *The Letters of Hannah More* (1925) p 163

[29] Alfred Gregory, *Robert Raikes: Journalist and Philanthropist* (1880) p 87

[30] Charlotte M. Yonge, *Hannah More* (1888) p 93

[31] More, op cit p 183

[32] Thomas Bernard, *Of the Education of the Poor* (1809) p 113

[33] John Foster, *Report of the Society for Bettering the Condition of the Poor* Vol I 1811 p 179

[34] Earl of Winchelsea, ibid. Vol I 1811 p 45

[35] Charles Birchenough, *History of Elementary Education in England and Wales* (1927) p 41

[36] *Gloucester Journal* 9 March, 1789; 23 March, 1789

[37] *Plans of the Sunday Schools & School of Industry established in Bath* (1789) p viii

[38] Ibid p 20

[39] Ibid p 28

[40] Ibid

[41] A charity school 'was a school confined to the poor and maintained by the relatively rich' (see Joan Simon 'Was there a Charity School Movement?' *Education in Leicestershire 1540–1940* (1968) p 62) but only those charity schools in which reading, writing and arithmetic were taught are included here.

[42] *Gloucester Journal* 27 October, 1788

[43] Thomas Bernard, *Report of the Society for Bettering the Condition of the Poor* Vol III 1802 p 30

[44] Thomas Bernard, *Education of the Poor* (1809) pp 15, 16

[45] *Gloucester Journal* 15 May, 1786

[46] H. C. Barnard, *A History of English Education* (1964) p 6

[47] J. W. Adamson, *A Short History of Education* (1919) pp 201, 203

[48] Thomas Bernard, *Education of the Poor* (1809) pp 12, 13, 14

[49] Ibid p 17

[50] T. D. Fosbrooke, *The original history of the City of Gloucester* (1819) p 436

[51] *Dymock Charity School Register Book*

[52] *Gloucester Journal* 8 November, 1779. Collections from sermons for the benefit of charity schools in Birmingham amounted to £112 4s 10d. See also *Gloucester Journal* 16 July, 1792 and 14 January, 1793

[53] Ibid 28 May, 1792

[54] Sarah Trimmer, *Reflections upon the Education of Children in Charity Schools* (1792) p 12

[55] Ibid p 13

[56] Thomas Paine, *Rights of Man* (Edited H. P. Bonner) (1937) p 127

[57] Ibid p 194

[58] Ibid p 195

[59] Ibid pp 220, 221

[60] Ibid p 224

[61] Ibid

[62] Ibid p 245

[63] *Leicester Journal* 7 November, 1792

[64] *Gloucester Journal* 31 December, 1792

[65] Ibid 14 January, 1793

[66] Graham Wallas, *Life of Francis Place* (1898) p 25

[67] J. H. Harris, *Robert Raikes: The Man who Founded the Sunday School* p 93

[68] More, op cit p 182

[69] T. R. Malthus, *First Essay on Population 1798* (reprinted 1966) p 11

[70] Ibid p 14

[71] Ibid pp 99, 100

[72] T. R. Malthus, *An Essay on Population* (1803, reprinted 1926) Vol 2 p 212

[73] Ibid

[74] S. E. Maltby, *Manchester and the Movement for National Elementary Education 1800–1870* (1918) p 18

[75] *Parliamentary Debates* (Hansard) Vol VIII p 867 19 February, 1807

[76] Ibid Vol IX p 1051 4 August, 1807

[77] Harriet Martineau, *A History of Thirty Years Peace* (1877) Vol I p 117

[78] Hansard, op cit Vol IX p 804 13 July, 1807

[79] Ibid p 800

[80] Ibid pp 798, 799

[81] Kay-Shuttleworth's letter to the Old Scholars of the Bamford Sunday School, 1867, quoted by Frank Smith, *The Life and Work of Sir James Kay-Shuttleworth* (1923) p 6

[82] Raikes, *Letter* 5 July, 1794

[83] H. B. Binns, *A Century of Education 1808–1908* (1908) p 6

[84] *The Imperial Magazine* (1828) 'Memoir of Robert Raikes Esq' p 402

[85] J. Lancaster, *Outlines of a Plan for Educating Ten Thousand Poor Children; Edinburgh Review* Vol II October, 1807 pp 69, 70

[86] *Quarterly Review* Vol 8 September, 1812 p 6

[87] W. J. Baker, *Henry Ryder: The First Evangelical Bishop; Bristol and Gloucestershire Archaeological Transactions* (1970) p 140

[88] A. Platts and G. H. Hainton, *Education in Gloucestershire: A Short History* (1953) p 55

[89] Andrew Bell, *Mutual Tuition and Moral Discipline* (1823) p 33

[90] *Gloucester Journal* 17 January, 1780

[91] M. G. Jones, *The Charity School Movement* (1938) p 314

[92] *Memoirs of Richard Lovell Edgeworth* begun by himself and concluded by his daughter Maria Edgeworth, Vol II Ireland 1969 p 461

[93] *Gloucester Journal* 4 August, 1788

[94] Smith, op cit pp 59, 60
[95] Joseph Stratford, *Good and Great Men of Gloucestershire* p 278
[96] *Gloucester Journal* 5 November, 1792
[97] Raikes, *Letter* 12 July, 1787
[98] J. H. Harris (editor), *Robert Raikes: The Man and his Work* pp 128, 129
[99] *Gloucester Journal* 27 August, 1792
[100] Ibid 16 July, 1792

Chapter 7

ROBERT RAIKES: THE MAN

The extravagant and adulatory language used about Raikes has tended to disguise for us the real man, as exampled by Thomas Bailey's *Eulogium*, 'gentle spirit of Raikes. . . . Whilst the approbation of the enlightened and virtuous of every age, the benedictions of grateful millions, the applause of posterity, the diffusion of knowledge, the extension of happiness, and the conversion of thousands from the paths of sin and death, to those of peace and holiness, shall form a monument to thy fame, which shall endure when the stately mausoleum and animated statue shall have mouldered in the dust; when the verse which sings the praise of princes, or the page which recounts the exploits of greatness, shall be heard only as an idle tale, or lost in the revolution of ages; a monument, which shall exist with the duration of human intellect, and crown thy head with a glory effulgent as the sun, and lasting as the throne of Omnipotence.'[1] Raikes saved himself possible embarrassment by dying four years before this appeared in print.

The purpose of this final chapter is to re-examine primary sources available: Raikes' newspaper reports, his letters, and the evidence of the few people who claimed to have known him, to determine if, or how, markedly different Raikes actually was from his 'public image'.

Raikes was a tough businessman, fully aware of the precariousness of eighteenth century existence for the impoverished many. As his father had done he made sure that he and his family enjoyed the security, comfort and delights of the well off. Raikes' chief concerns were the support and well-being of his wife and family, his business, particularly the editorship of his newspaper, and his duties as a churchman.

It was characteristic of Raikes to be shrewd and diligent in business affairs. He was reliable, respected, trusted and prosperous, but his work must have proved demanding both of his time and energy. When the day of the publication of the *Gloucester*

Journal was changed from Tuesday to Monday, Raikes was obliged to devote part of Sunday to editing the following day's copy – hence the accusation that it was the noise made by rowdy children outside his office which bestirred him to have them removed to Sunday school. His business was not free from problems and worry: in his correspondence in 1790 he complained, 'I have had so many obstructions from the sickness of some and the idleness of others of my men that I have been under the greatest distress to get thro' my business.'[2] On one occasion because of the incompetence of one of his employees Raikes was fined; an advertisement appeared in the *Gloucester Journal* offering 'five guineas reward and no questions asked', but the making of this offer was illegal under an old Act of Parliament, and carried a £50 penalty. Raikes claimed that the notice had been printed in his newspaper during his absence in London; nonetheless he had to pay the fine. 'My compositor was ignorant of this law, and inserted the advertisement as it was sent. And now I am compelled by an infamous pettyfogging lawyer to pay this sum for my servant's ignorance.'[3]

Relationships with his workers were not always harmonious, but perhaps Raikes was not always a very understanding employer. William Whitehead, one of Raikes' apprentices, described his employer as 'very strict in all his business matters'.[4] Raikes certainly blackguarded an eighteen year old apprentice who absconded from his service. The following notice appeared in the *Gloucester Journal*, 18 August, 1788. 'RUNAWAY APPRENTICE: WHEREAS JOHN JONES, Apprentice to R. Raikes, has left his service without provocation; – this is to forewarn all persons from entertaining or employing him, as they will be prosecuted with the utmost vigour of the law. JOHN JONES is nearly 19 years of age, strait brown hair, about five feet seven inches high, wore a light drab coat, with a black collar, a cross barred waistcoat, and leather breeches – The public must be cautious how they trust him.' Often when an apprentice ran away the employer in the advertisement promised kind treatment and no notice to be taken of the incident if the youngster returned immediately, but Raikes offered no such reconciliation. In the next issue of his paper Raikes again severely condemned the lad and gave no hint of Christian forgiveness. 'The public are cautioned to beware of JOHN JONES, a run-away apprentice, advertised last week, who has been hiring horses, and borrowing money under various pretences. He was last seen at Brecon, and said he was going to an uncle in Cardiganshire. – Beware of this fellow, for he has lost all sense of truth and honesty.'[5] Even if Raikes were upset, he was very hard on the young man. There is no evidence that the apprentice ever returned to Raikes' employ. To be strictly fair to Raikes, however, it should be made clear that the youngster was breaking the law.

In business Raikes invariably knew where advantage lay. In his letters to his client, the Revd William Lewellyn, of Leominster, Raikes suggested that letters to him should be addressed to Mr John Pitt, MP for Gloucester, thereby avoiding the payment of postal charges.[6] When this was not possible Raikes made alternative arrangements of a similar kind when on 27 January, 1792, he advised, 'As my friend Mr Pitt is going to London to attend Parliament please direct your next letter to Samuel Woodcock Esq., Postmaster Gloucester.'[7]

Through his work as a newspaper editor Raikes encountered many examples of the havoc being wrought in the lives of common people by the revolutions taking place in agriculture, industry and commerce. He also knew that, even had he so wished, he would have been powerless to change the immovable political, social, economic and religious structures which dominated eighteenth century English society. To his credit, like others of the press, he applauded in the columns of his newspaper acts of benevolence and virtue, and, circumspectly, attacked selfishness, heartlessness and vice.

Raikes' editorial comment when reporting the outcome of a prize fight in London where a Colonel Tarleton was one of the umpires and Lord Barrymore, the Duke of Bedford and the Duke of Queensbury were 'the leaders of the assembly', indicated clearly Raikes' dislike of such contests, the behaviour exhibited and the examples set. 'It is conjectured, 4,000 people were collected, and such horrid blasphemies, confusion, and noise rent the air, such quarrelling and fighting among the low, such disputing among the high, that whatever might be deemed shocking and disgraceful to rational beings, whatever might be conceived likely to introduce disorder and brutality into this kingdom, was there to be seen, patronised and encouraged.'[8]

The roles for which Raikes became famous – those of prison

visitor and founder of Sunday schools – were initially only inci-
dental to his way of life, yet he learned from them that human
happiness depends upon mutual sympathy, although his own
behaviour was very ambivalent. His sympathy was aroused by
those imprisoned for debt in Gloucester gaol, as instanced in the
following case of the sad misfortunes of a farmer. 'The fire that
broke out the 18th of March last (1783) at the lone farm, called
Cock Harbour Farm in the parish of South Littleton, was very
fatal, as it consumed the farm-house, barns, stables, cowhouses,
and every part of the buildings (with a large quantity of corn and
household goods, &c.) to the amount of £700 and upwards,
which falls on a man who cannot support the loss; and to add to
the poor man's misfortunes, he was very soon after arrested by
his pretended friend, and now lies in jail in great distress. It is to
be hoped that charitable well-disposed people will contribute
towards his loss. The fire was occasioned by a boy shooting some
sparrows.'[9] The active, purposeful Raikes did not just express sorrow, he invoked public sympathy by reporting in his newspaper
the condition of the debtors and readily agreed to act as agent to
receive and ensure the proper distribution of gifts sent for the
alleviation of the prisoners' distress.

Raikes, who read widely himself, believed that reading was an
important civilising force and he continued his interest in prisoners being taught to read. His editorial in the *Gloucester Journal* 20
August, 1787 shows this. 'A few days ago, the three young men
whom the magistrates of this city, sentenced at the last sessions,
for riotous behaviour, when in liquor, to a month's confinement
in solitude were set at large. This wholesome chastisement, it is
hoped, may leave a lasting impression upon minds, that were
discovered far from intractable. When they entered into confinement they scarcely knew their letters, but by the good natured
assistance of a man in the prison, in intervals from labour, they
made considerable progress towards reading . . . From the good
resolutions with which these men appeared to quit the prison, it
should seem consequences the most beneficial may be expected . . .'

On the other hand Raikes' attitude to felons was the same,
generally speaking, as that held by most of his contemporaries.
Examples of their suffering should be made public as a deterrent
to others. In spite of the brutality of the law Raikes never even

suggested, let alone attempted, any measure of law reform. He simply gave full publicity to the dire consequences for those convicted of breaking the law. He was not squeamish in reporting executions and when 'six malefactors were executed' in Gloucester in April, 1788, he described the sickening details of the criminals' last moments, obviously to deter any who might risk the same punishment, rather than for the interest of his readers. 'Collins was a long time in dying; he struggled in great agonies. From his nose the blood gushed forth, running down his cloathes in a copious stream.' Raikes probably prevailed upon one of the criminals, Francis Turner, aged 24, to address the crowd around the gallows. (It was a common enough practice.) 'You, young ones, let me exhort you to avail yourselves of the opportunity now afforded, of learning your duty by means of Sunday Schools – Had I been early taught this important lesson, Keep holy the Sabbath Day, you had not seen me in this distress – But when I was a lad; Sunday Schools were not thought of.'[10] Turner would have been sixteen when Raikes and Stock opened their Sunday schools. Turner was hanged for horse stealing and the other five for housebreaking.

Of course thievery and robbery were rife, and propertied people spared little pity for those suffering punishment under the law. Raikes himself appears to have been held up during one of his visits to London. 'On Thursday last, as Mr Raikes and his daughter, of Alderman's Walk, London, were passing through Maidenhead Thicket, in their road to town, about eight o'clock in the evening, the chaise was stopped by three footpads, who robbed them of their purses and pocket-books.'[11]

We do not find Raikes in his consideration of all prisoners the 'gentle spirit' as described in Bailey's *Eulogium*. Whether or not he knew the master and apprentice referred to in the following case reported in the *Gloucester Journal* is not ascertainable, but there is no sympathy in the judgement he felt entitled to make on the apprentice. Indeed this was not the only time Raikes went 'beyond the law' in personally condemning a prisoner in his newspaper. 'John Boughton, apprentice to Mr Squire, staymaker of this city, was convicted not only of robbing his master of his property, but of attempting to calumniate the character of his mistress; and though the jury brought in a verdict of petit larceny, yet the judge sentenced the wretch to transportation for seven years: and if the goods stolen could have been sworn to, there is no doubt but the villain would have been hanged, as he richly deserved.'[12]

However, Raikes had sympathy for some who were convicted, although often he could do little for them. Since there were few people like himself willing to help in rehabilitating prisoners, many were discharged from jail without means of support, jobless and friendless. 'Richard Henley was sentenced at our assizes to be whipped. The punishment was on Monday last inflicted with such severity, that his back was almost flead; yet on Wednesday he was brought back to prison for stealing a scythe, and other tools. He says he is an inhabitant of Temple Street, Bristol. Having been discharged without the means of procuring any sustenance, he declares he was compelled to steal by extreme hunger.'[13] On one occasion Raikes successfully petitioned a judge to spare the life of a man convicted of sheep stealing. Caroline, Raikes' youngest daughter, recalled that the man, having been transported to Botany Bay, started a Sunday school there.[14]

In advocating prison reform Raikes was concerned to protect the health of prisoners, but not to suggest that life in prison should be made more than tolerable. He warned wrongdoers, for instance, what conditions would be like in Gloucester's new prison. 'The terrifying aspect of the New Prison begins already to manifest its effects. Tho' June is half expired, no culprit has been committed since its commencement. The cells for confinement in solitude are many of them nearly finished, and dreary indeed will be the fate of those, who are doomed to inhabit them.'[15]

Though Raikes was undoubtedly insensitive in these pronouncements, his chief social objectives were the prevention of crime and disorder, and he frequently attacked what he considered to be their root causes, namely, immorality, vice, idleness, mendicity and vagrancy. As a newspaper editor he was fully conversant with the current expense involved in paying for all the paraphernalia of the law, and as a land-owner and ratepayer Raikes' interest in this was very specific. No tenderness or kindly understanding can be attributed to Raikes on these issues; he constantly applauded the severest measures. Raikes included financial justification of action taken against three (presumably sturdy) beggars. 'On Wednesday last three vagrants, in the garb of sailors, who were begging in the streets of this city, were taken up, and after a severe flogging thro' the streets, were dismissed with a recommendation to betake themselves to a better mode of obtaining a livelihood, for the same treatment will be given to all persons of their description who visit this city. If the magistrates in every county and city in the kingdom, would act in the same spirit, the number of vagrants would be diminished, and immense charges saved.' The expenses to the county for dealing with 'passing vagrants' according to the treasurer's accounts for 1788 had been £773 17s., but Raikes reported, 'by the new regulations established by the Justices, we understand this item is likely to be reduced near £500'.[16]

Having helped to clear the streets of unruly children Raikes was himself intolerant of adults who set a bad example to the young and he gave his unequivocal approval to the decisive, vigorous action taken by the authorities against those caught indulging in antisocial behaviour. 'On Saturday evening,' reported Raikes, 'a man who called himself James Dee, was committed to one of the cells of the city prison for ten days, being convicted of swearing several prophane oaths. – The thanks of the public are highly due to the Magistrates who enforce laws made for the maintenance of decency and good morals – Behaviour disgraceful to civil society, is not suffered here to escape with impunity.'[17]

The adoption of attitudes towards miscreants which would be unacceptable to most of us today, should not lead us to the immediate conclusion that Raikes was totally unsympathetic to those who infringed the law, or whose behaviour he disliked. On the contrary it required a courageous and sympathetic nature to take the risks involved in visiting Gloucester Castle Gaol, where Raikes knew there was always the chance of contagion from highly virulent diseases, such as smallpox and gaol fever, as well as some danger of injury by personal contact with persons whom it was known could be extremely violent. Perhaps the frequent harshness of Raikes' responses was to some extent attributable to his experience in dealing with prisoners, since not all, especially those under sentence of death, behaved, to use Raikes' own words, 'with decency and resignation'.

The greatest tribute that can be paid to Raikes is the sympathy he extended to neglected children. Raikes exhibited both Christian spirit and strength of personality in visiting the parents in their homes and persuading them to send their children to Sunday school. He was fortunate, in that, having found willing teachers to take charge of the children, he could have abdicated from the situation at any time if the strain proved too testing, but apparently this was not the case. Raikes was relied on as the ultimate authority to whom the teachers turned to discipline the most truculent scholars.

Raikes was a well-known and trusted public figure in his own city. He was a member of the Vestry of the parish of St Mary de Crypt, a trustee of the Mary Shaile Charity, which distributed funds annually to the poor within that parish, one of the eight Vice-Presidents of the Severn Humane Society, and, in 1788, a joint trustee of the Gloucester Provident Society. The list is by no means complete. As Raikes was regarded as one of Gloucester's leading citizens it must have taken a great deal of courage and determination on his part to ignore the jeers of those who called him 'crank' and to lead his 'ragged regiment' of Sunday school scholars through the streets to church.

Samuel William Riley (1759–1837), an actor befriended by Raikes, left us this description of him: 'Oft have I seen this philanthropic being walk to church at seven in the morning, follow'd by at least an hundred children, who, but for him, might have lived and died in ignorance, with all its attendant vices. The clergy, strange to say! opposed him; the people scarcely approved the plan, or lent assistance to its success.'[18] In view of Riley's words it would seem that Raikes needed both grit and tenacity to carry on.

It is for his vision, however, more than any other characteristic, that Raikes should be remembered. He recognised, before any of his contemporaries, that Sunday schools had a tremendous potential as agencies for social change. 'A reformation in society seems to me,' he wrote in his first letter about Sunday schools, 'only practicable by establishing notices of duty, and practical habits of order and decorum, at an early stage . . . Let our patriots employ themselves in rescuing their countrymen from that despotism, which tyrannical passions and vicious inclinations exercise over them, and they will find that true liberty and national welfare are more essentially promoted, than by any reform in Parliament.'[19]

Raikes was predicting, to use his own words written six years later, 'a radical cure' of social ills by applying 'every means that tend to humanize and mold the character in its early formation'.

Children should be 'rescued' by educating them. The instruction of the young, as Raikes conceived it, was not simply coercive and repressive in order to subordinate the poor, although his educational outlook in respect of them involved submissiveness, respectfulness and subordination to 'their betters'. Vitally important, again to use his own words, was the implanting of 'seeds of knowledge, virtue and probity, in the season of youth, when the soil is fittest to receive them.'[20]

It would have been futile to rely upon the government of the day to take action. The concern of MP's for the poor was exactly reflected in the business of the House of Commons as reported in the *Gloucester Journal* of 21 April, 1788. 'On Thursday 17th April, Mr Gilbert moved that his bill for the relief of the poor be now read a second time. Mr Young (argued) that instead of "now" the words "this day three months" be inserted. In favour of the amendment Ayes 44 Noes 10 Majority for rejecting the Bill 34.' Only fifty-four members took part in the voting yet the next day when the House divided on a naval issue two hundred and eighty-three members were present and voted. Civil authorities, according to Raikes, had an important duty in adopting 'a vigilant and active polity, particularly in the suppression and restraint of those places of idle resort (alehouses) where bad propensities not only expand themselves, but become infectious.'[21] The responsibility for social reform must rest, however, with individuals sympathetic to the needs and welfare of their neighbours. 'These patriots', so named by Raikes, were to be found among the ranks of the well-to-do: men like William Fox and Samuel Webb and women such as Sarah Trimmer and the More sisters. All those with time and energy, who were sufficiently well educated to help and advise common people, especially the paid Sunday school teachers, might be persuaded to help.

Raikes was obviously delighted to give publicity to interest taken in Sunday schools and to any special contributions made to their work by members of the aristocracy. The Sunday schools at Nympsfield, Gloucestershire, had been established in 1784 for 'upwards of 100 children' and to encourage them in good behaviour, Lady Ducie gave them 'a Sunday dinner of beef and pudding'.[22] Sunday schools at St Albans under the patronage 'of the benevolent Dowager Lady Spencer are excellently regulated', reported Raikes in 1789. 'Her ladyship visits the schools herself, is regular in attending at eight in the morning, and does not get home to dinner till five, during which time she teaches the scholars, and twice goes to church. At eight in the evening she has her servants into prayers which she reads herself. A striking example for other ladies of rank to follow.'[23]

Himself a staunch churchman, Raikes saw the Church as the centre of the spiritual life of the nation and those in holy orders as its spiritual and moral leaders. The instruction and welfare of the people, particularly the young, he regarded as the responsibility of the clergy, hence he naturally first discussed the founding of Sunday schools in Gloucester with a clergyman, the Revd Thomas Stock, who had experience of working with children on Sundays. To Raikes, perhaps more than anyone else, should go the credit for arousing the Church from its apathy and worldliness to attend to this mission.

Unfortunately there seems to have been some estrangement between Raikes and the local clergy. In 1787 Raikes complained, 'Within this month the minister of my parish has, at last, condescended to give me assistance in this laborious work (supervision of the Sunday schools) which I have carried on six years with little or no support.'[24] And again in 1790 he wrote 'alas! now nobody regards the design. I work alone'.[25]

Raikes appears to have suffered from an inability to share the public acclaim he received. One of his critics, the Revd Arthur B. Evans, who had been under-master at the Cathedral School, Gloucester, when the Revd Thomas Stock was headmaster, wrote of Raikes in 1831, 'unfortunately an excessive vanity was a prominent feature of Mr Raikes's character, a circumstance in which you will find all his surviving contemporaries uniformily agree. He was otherwise a good natured, hospitable man, doing the honours of the place to any conspicuous strangers who visited it.'[26] Never once in the *Gloucester Journal* did Raikes mention the labours of his co-worker, Thomas Stock, in supervising the Gloucester Sunday schools, or indeed the work of his brother the Revd Richard Raikes. On the occasion of one of the visits of Prince William, Duke of Gloucester, to Raikes' house, Richard, noting that his brother had omitted to mention the part taken by the Revd Thomas Stock, commented, 'Never mind: my brother has his reward on earth: Mr Stock will have his in Heaven.'[27]

According to the Revd A. B. Evans, Raikes and Stock together established the first Sunday school in the house of James King, Mrs King being engaged as the mistress. They then set up two other Sunday schools in the parish of St Catherine. The expense was shared jointly, two thirds being met by Raikes and one third by Stock. However, contended Evans, 'When Mr. Raikes established a similar School in his own parish of St. Mary de Crypt, he discontinued his contribution to the Schools in St Catherine's, and the expenditure then fell intirely upon Mr. Stock, until at a future period, the Rev. Richard Raikes came to reside in Gloucester, and took a share in the expense. When Mr Stock became curate of St. John's and St. Aldate's, he established two Sunday schools in his own parish at his own expense, in Hare-Lane.

'The circumstance of Mr. Raikes's discontinuing his contribution to the St. Catherine School, has been confirmed to me by Mr. Stock's widow, now residing in Gloucester, who well remembers her husband's complaining of the additional pecuniary burden laid upon him.'[28]

Stock certainly should be accorded credit for the founding, supervision and support of Sunday schools in Gloucester, and also for the sermons he preached for the benefit of Sunday schools in both the city and the county. A sincere, devout and learned cleric, Stock was stressing publicly in 1795, 'the necessity of cultivating religious principles, as the only sure and permanent foundation for the maintenance and support of order and good government in Society.'[29] He died in 1803 at the age of 54 years.

Raikes' reluctance to share honours with Stock apparently hurt his friend. G. W. Counsel, a well-known local antiquary (already quoted) who had known Raikes and Stock intimately, wrote in 1841, 'Mr. Raikes contributed to the establishment of Sunday Schools by giving publicity to the same through the medium of the Gloucester Journal. I well remember that Mr. Stock appeared much hurt at Mr. Raikes' being styled in that paper "The Founder of Sunday Schools."'[30] However, since Raikes never mentioned his own name in his newspaper in connection with Sunday schools, perhaps G. W. Counsel was referring to articles in the *Gentleman's Magazine* or other papers.

Raikes has been described as being highly emotional on at least two occasions. During a visit to his house by a student, Charles H. Wilton, just prior to his departure to Naples to study the violin, Raikes took him into his garden. Having closed the door and taken his young friend's arm, Raikes is said to have 'burst into tears, and was for some time unable to give vent to his feelings'. At length he appears to have exclaimed, '"Oh, God! what am I, that thou shouldest make me the instrument of saving a soul from death? I had a dream, Charles, last night, by which I feel assured that this meeting is by the appointment of heaven. Let me, therefore, request that you will, in your way to your father's, call at some booksellers and get, or order immediately, 'Gilpin on the Catechism.' Retire for half an hour every day, and read a portion of it; and may the Lord bless it to your eternal welfare."' [31]

A Dr Kennedy, of Connecticut, described an incident during the meeting of Raikes and Joseph Lancaster as follows. Raikes, then an old man, was leaning on the arm of his young acquaintance as they walked. 'When they reached a certain place, the elder of the two said, "Pause here," and so saying he uncovered his brow, closed his eyes, and stood for a moment in silent prayer . . . and the tears rolled down his cheeks as he said to his friend, "This is the spot on which I stood when I saw the destitution of the children, and the desecration of the Sabbath by the inhabitants of the town; and I asked, 'Can nothing be done?' and a voice answered, 'Try,' and I did try, and see what God hath wrought! I can never pass by the spot where the word 'try' came so powerfully into my mind without lifting up my hands and heart to heaven in gratitude to God for having put such a thought into my heart."' [32]

Whatever his affectations and shortcomings, Raikes had the ability to interest, entertain, and influence people. In his home and city he proved a pleasing host. Notable visitors to Gloucester were entertained by him and people came to expect a genial welcome and generosity from him. At least one Sunday school founder believed Raikes to be approachable and helpful. Unable to afford the coach fare, James Kemp, a poor shoemaker, walked from Hoxton, London, to Gloucester to see Raikes to learn from him how his Sunday schools were conducted.

Raikes was skilful in interesting and influencing his Sunday school children. The lasting effect of his personal influence is perhaps best portrayed in the story of Jack Pelham, a cabin boy, whom the ship's crew nicknamed 'Jack Raikes'. This former Sunday school scholar was a very devout Christian and during a voyage, at his own request, he nursed and ministered to one of the

sailors who was in the death throes of a fever. Unfortunately the
ship foundered on a rock during a violent storm and the lifeboat
with young Pelham in overturned and he was drowned. The next
day his body was washed ashore and amongst his possessions
was found a Bible and engraved on its brass clips were the words
'The gift of Robert Raikes to Jack Pelham'.

Not only could Raikes entertain strangers and interest and
influence children, he could also entertain an idea. The idea that
the children of the poorest of the nation's families should and
could be educated was revolutionary, but Raikes conceived it as a
practicality, applied it, and popularised it. Raikes had great ability
as a publicist, and frequently drew such convincing comparisons
as: 'Few require to be informed that the morals of the lower class
of people . . . are in a state of barbarous ignorance and abandoned profligacy', set against the change brought about by Sunday school attendance: 'Their behaviour bears testimony of the
good effects of this instruction. In church, which they constantly
frequent, they behave with great order and decorum, and in the
whole of their conduct, they are greatly humanised and seem
very desirous to learn.'[33] The whole nation owed the inception of
tremendous changes to Raikes' ability to imbue others with his
enthusiasm which resulted in the establishment of Sunday
schools throughout the kingdom. The accuracy of John Richard
Green's statement in his work *A Short History of the English People*:
'The Sunday Schools established by Mr Raikes of Gloucester at
the close of the century were the beginnings of popular education', has still to be fully appreciated.

Schools for poor children were supported by all ranks of society
and helped 'humanise' all the participants. Although nearly
another half-century was to elapse before many cruel laws were
radically altered, the nation gradually awakened to the need to
instruct the poor. Raikes' frequent call for the 'most melancholy
reflections' upon the 'extreme youth' of criminals, as instanced by
such sentences as those imposed in 1789, 'Out of nine, who were
cast for death at the Old Bailey . . . two were only 20, two of
them 18, one of 14 and the youngest 12 years of age',[34] was iterated in charity sermons preached on behalf of Sunday schools
and weekday schools. The Revd Thomas Lloyd, in a sermon calling for support of St Mary's Charity School, Leicester, declared,
'The present very corrupt state of the poor is truly alarming . . .

and nothing is to be expected but an increase in depravity.' He emphasised the inadequacy of the legislature to deal with the problem and the ineffectiveness of the penal code with all its severity, and continued, 'It may dismember society, in order to preserve its interest; it may depopulate in order to purify our country. Yet this remedy, how desperate, how little preferable to the disease! To see justice (as we have seen her) unsheathing her sword of vengeance against multitudes of our fellow citizens, dealing deaths around and destroying almost as largely as war itself does, is a scene truly distressing.'[35] Sunday schools and day schools for the poor saved vast numbers of the subjects of George III from the barbarity of the law.

Some idea of the progress of popular education can be gained by comparing an estimate referred to by Sarah Trimmer in 1786, that 40,000 children were attending charity schools (the only day schools where the children of the common people who could not afford to pay for the instruction of their children might attend), with the figures contained in the 1818 Parliamentary returns. These figures showed that in England and Wales there were purported to be, by 1818, '19,230 day schools containing 674,883 scholars (a majority of whom would be children attending charity schools), being 1 in 17.25 of the population, and 5,463 Sunday schools containing 477,225 scholars or 1 in 24.40 of the population.'[36]

Raikes too had the wisdom to see that the nature of the schooling was important, believing as he did that children should learn to read and speak intelligibly, thereby having access to knowledge through the Bible, the Church, and, of course, newspapers. To some of the illiterate poor, Sunday schools and charity schools meant much more than this. For them a latent potential was realised. They acquired identity, intellect, dignity, and understanding – a new salvation.

After many years of service to Sunday schools Robert Raikes, who might well be judged the 'Founder of the Sunday School Movement', died quite suddenly only half an hour after complaining of pains in his chest, on 5 April, 1811, aged 74. Sunday school children followed the cortege to the grave and, in accordance with his instructions, received a shilling and a plum cake. He was buried in the same vault as his father in the Church of St Mary de Crypt.

NOTES

[1] T. Bailey, *An Eulogium on the Character of Mr Robert Raikes* (1815)

[2] Raikes, *Letter* 9 April, 1790

[3] Ibid 27 April, 1792

[4] J. H. Harris (editor), *Robert Raikes: The Man and his Work* p 188

[5] *Gloucester Journal* 25 August, 1788

[6] Raikes, *Letter* 23 October, 1791: 'This I should receive free of postage.'

[7] Ibid 27 January, 1792. See also Raikes, *Letter* 6 February, 1792

[8] *Gloucester Journal* 22 February, 1790

[9] Ibid 21 April, 1783

[10] Ibid 21 April, 1788

[11] Ibid 3 March, 1788

[12] Ibid 3 April, 1786

[13] Ibid 10 April, 1786

[14] Caroline Weller-Ladbroke's *Letter* 27 December, 1862 quoted Harris, op cit pp 207, 208

[15] *Gloucester Journal* 15 June, 1789

[16] Ibid 14 December, 1789

[17] Ibid 8 September, 1788

[18] S. W. Riley, *The Itinerant; or Memoirs of an Actor* (1817) Vol I

[19] Raikes, *Letter* 25 November, 1783

[20] *Gloucester Journal* 7 December, 1789

[21] Ibid

[22] Ibid 11 October, 1784

[23] Ibid 20 July, 1789

[24] Raikes, *Letter* 5 November, 1787

[25] Ibid 8 November, 1793

[26] Arthur B. Evans, *Letter; Gentleman's Magazine* October 1831 p 295

[27] Henry Wintle, Rector of Matson, Gloucester, 1841; quoted H. Y. J. Taylor *Collection of Newspaper Articles and Letters* Gloucester City Library Vol 14315

[28] *Gentleman's Magazine* October 1831 p 295

[29] *Gloucester Journal* 12 October, 1795

[30] Ibid 15 May, 1841

[31] *The Sunday School Teachers' Magazine* 1830 p 682

[32] Joseph Stratford, *Robert Raikes and Others: The Founders of Sunday Schools* (1880) p 105

[33] *Gloucester Journal* 11 October, 1784

[34] Ibid 14 December, 1789

[35] T. Lloyd, *A sermon preached in the Parish of St. Mary, Leicester* 1787

[36] W. H. Watson, *The First Fifty Years of the Sunday Schools* p 112

INDEX